WATG – Studio N

DETAIL Praxis

Translucent Materials

Glass
Plastics
Metals

Frank Kaltenbach (Ed.)

Birkhäuser
Edition Detail

Authors:
Andrea Compagno, Dipl.-Ing.
Joachim Achenbach, Dipl.-Ing.
Werner Sobek, Prof. Dr.-Ing.
Lucio Blandini, Dipl.-Ing.
Frank Maier, Dipl.-Ing.
Jan Knippers, Prof. Dr.-Ing.
Stefan Peters, Dipl.-Ing.
Frank Kaltenbach, Dipl.-Ing.
Karsten Moritz, Dipl.-Ing.
Rainer Barthel, Prof. Dr.-Ing.
Stefan Schäfer, Prof. Dipl.-Ing.
Manfred Gränzer, Dr.-Ing.

Editor:
Frank Kaltenbach, Dipl.-Ing.

Editorial team:
Heike Werner, Dipl.-Ing.
Christos Chantzaras, cand. Arch.

Translation German/English:
Michael Robinson

DTP & production:
Peter Gensmantel, Cornelia Kohn, Andrea Linke,
Roswitha Siegler

© 2004 Institut für internationale
Architektur-Dokumentation GmbH & Co.KG,
P.O.Box 33 06 60, D–80066 Munich, Germany

ISBN 3-7643-7033-5

Printed on acid-free paper, manufactured from
chlorine-free bleached cellulose.

Printed by:
Wesel-Kommunikation,
Baden-Baden

A CIP catalogue record for this book is available
from the Library of Congress, Washington, D.C.,
USA

Bibliographic information published by Die
Deutsche Bibliothek
Die Deutsche Bibliothek lists this publication in
the Deutsche Nationalbibliografie; detailed
bibliographic data is available on the internet at
http://dnb.ddb.de

Institut für internationale
Architektur-Dokumentation GmbH & Co.KG
Sonnenstrasse 17, D-80331 Munich
Tel. +49 89 38 16 20-0
Fax +49 89 39 86 70
e-mail: vertrieb@detail.de
Internet: www.detail.de

Distribution Partner:
Birkhäuser – Publishers for Architecture
P.O.Box 133, CH-4010 Basel,
Switzerland
Tel. +41 61 205 07 07
Fax +41 61 205 07 92
e-mail: sales@birkhauser.ch
http://www.birkhauser.ch

DETAIL Praxis
Translucent Materials

Contents

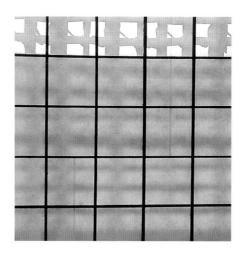

"…we Japanese fit additional canopies or verandas outside rooms that the rays of the sun in any case penetrate only with difficulty. This is to keep out even more light and ensure that only a diffuse reflection can steal in from the garden through the paper windows. So the aesthetic element in our rooms is nothing other that this indirect, dim lighting effect."

from: "In Praise of Shadow"
Tanizaki Jun'chiro

Translucency –
Light made material

In recent years, many architects have not just wanted to create exciting spaces: they have also shown a particular interest in surface design, in tactile properties, colour and texture. Façades are sensitively enhanced, becoming artistic structures that enter into an unusual dialogue with their surroundings, based on their degree of abstraction. Translucent materials are available that make it possible to work with daylight even behind such homogeneous envelopes. From the outside, they create an even appearance despite all the irregularities of the shell, but at the same time admit light to the interior and – where it is desirable or a legal requirement – make it possible to look out. The architectural theme is not the well-proportioned relationship of closed and open areas any longer, but the façade structure's ability to reflect and transmit light. Is architecture, in our increasingly virtual perception culture, shifting from the sensuality of material to the sensuality of light? The "free play of bodies in light", as Le Corbusier defined architecture, would then become the play of materialized light as a component of the dematerialized body of a building.

The word translucency is derived from the Latin "trans" (through) and "lux" (light), and means that light penetrates a material. Translucent materials are not the same as transparent ones, which can be seen through clearly as well as allowing light to pass. Translucent and transparent materials are categorized as diaphanous (Greek: showing through) materials.

Manipulating light has always had mystical associations. In prehistoric times, technical inadequacies made it impossible to see out clearly: animal skins were used at windows, for example. But translucent materials have featured in religious architecture from time immemorial. Mystery is often added to the holiest place in many churches by using thinly cut translucent panes of onyx, marble or alabaster. In the Gothic period, entire walls were dissolved into transcendental light by the use of glazed windows; the most consistent example of this is the Sainte Chapelle in Paris. Since the Enlightenment – the very word contains light – more transparent panes have increasingly been used in step with technical progress – banishing the "dark Middle Ages".

Light has always been modulated and windows shaded in oriental cultures. There textiles and paper are among the traditional translucent materials. Islamic façades are distinguished by so-called musharabîya – lattice-work, made of wrought iron, turned wood or carved natural stone according to region. The interplay of interior and exterior is particularly cultivated in Japanese architecture: when open, the translucent paper screens give direct access to nature, and closed they provide an opaque surface, glowing with light. This concept of fluid space has considerably influenced modern Western architecture since the early 20th century.

Frank Lloyd Wright designed his glazing intricately, like the Japanese paper screens. Perforated roof projections, coloured glass windows, pierced concrete block façades and skylights made of dully shimmering fibre-glass create a filter from light to dark. In contrast with this, Mies van der Rohe chose the largest possible clear panes for his buildings, to cancel the distinction between inside and outside completely. The single glazing that was customary at the time transmitted a great deal of light and energy in comparison with today's double or triple glazing, thus giving an impression of being in the open air.

And now architects, and interior and other designers, have new building materials at their disposal, ranging from completely transparent to almost opaquely translucent. These products do not just meet increasingly complex requirements and regulations, but provide a design potential that is still far from exhausted. A number of new finishing techniques have shown that glass is still a versatile material that can increasingly be used structurally, i.e. without any additional support. Plastic panels can now meet the necessary heat, sound and fire insulation requirements. Membranes are not just used as translucent tent roofs, but can be deployed in the form of highly transparent, ultra-light sheeting as almost invisible building envelopes. Translucent metallic semi-finished products are not just available as perforated sheet and expanded metals: a whole variety of meshes make it possible to bridge large spans and control the degree of translucency according to mesh size and weave.

Complex requirements can often not be met by one of these groups of materials alone. Glass is preferred to meet the highest standards in terms of building physics. Functions like solar screening, glare protection, sight-screening or creative requirements can be fulfilled by membranes or perforated metal sheeting. Composite products, exploiting the positive properties of several materials, are also becoming more common.

One major project clearly demonstrates the trend towards translucent materials. Highly transparent acrylic glass was chosen to cover the Olympic stadium roof in Munich in 1972, which was very much in tune with the idea of openness for the "happy games". But the "Witches' Cauldron", the stadium's successor building for the 2006 Football World Cup, will be closed, to intensify the mass experience. For the façade and roof covering, architects Herzog & de Meuron are going to use some translucent and some transparent ETFE cushions. They will be backlit at night, making them seem completely immaterial, and transforming the building into a glowing urban landmark.

Frank Kaltenbach

Authors:

Andrea Compagno, Dipl.-Ing. Architect, façade planning and consultation, Zurich
Department of Building Technology, Accademia di Architettura, Università della
Svizzera Italiana UNISI, Mendrisio and Visiting Professor, Illinois Institute of Technology, IIT, Chicago
www.compagno.ch

Joachim Achenbach, Dipl.-Ing. Architect
Free-lance architect, Stuttgart
www.achenbach-architekten.com

Werner Sobek, Prof. Dr.-Ing. Structural engineer
Institut für Leichtbau Entwerfen und Konstruieren (ILEK; Institute of Lightweight
Building Design and Construction), University of Stuttgart
www.uni-stuttgart.de/ilek

Lucio Blandini, Dipl.-Ing. Architect
Institut für Leichtbau Entwerfen und Konstruieren (ILEK; Institute of Lightweight
Building Design and Construction), University of Stuttgart
www.uni-stuttgart.de/ilek

Frank Maier, Dipl.-Ing.
Baden-Württemberg Office of Building Technology, specialist topics fire protection,
glass, engineering inspectors.
www.lgabw.de/lfb

Jan Knippers, Prof. Dr.-Ing.
Institut für Tragkonstruktionen und Konstruktives Entwerfen (ITKE; Institute of
Loadbearing Structures and Structural Design), University of Stuttgart
http://itke.architektur.uni-stuttgart.de

Stefan Peters, Dipl.-Ing.
Institut für Tragkonstruktionen und Konstruktives Entwerfen (ITKE; Institute of
Loadbearing Structures and Structural Design), University of Stuttgart
http://itke.architektur.uni-stuttgart.de

Frank Kaltenbach, Dipl.-Ing. Architekt
Technical editor for DETAIL magazine,
Institut für internationale Architektur-Dokumentation GmbH & Co. KG, Munich
www.detail.de

Karsten Moritz, Dipl.-Ing. Bauingenieur Dipl.-Ing. Architekt
Department of Load-bearing Structure Planning, Technische Universität Munich
www.lt.arch.tu-muenchen.de

Rainer Barthel, Prof. Dr.-Ing. Bauingenieur
Department of Load-bearing Structure Planning, Technische Universität Munich
www.lt.arch.tu-muenchen.de

Stefan Schäfer, Prof. Dipl.-Ing. Architekt
Institute of Masonry Wall Construction, Structural Design and Building Construction
section, Technische Universität Darmstadt,
www.massivbau.tu-darmstadt.de/konges/index.html

Manfred Gränzer, Dr.-Ing.
Director of the Baden-Württemberg Office of Building Technology
www.lgabw.de/lfb

Glass

Glass as a building material – Developments and trends

Andrea Compagno

Major progress in glass technology has given us a building material combining architectural, tectonic, economic and ecological advantages. These developments were triggered by the 70s oil crisis, when people were looking for a kind of glass architecture that could be less greedy of energy. The following survey shows the glass types available today and the ways in which they can be used. The innovation potential in this field is still by no means exhausted. For this reason, glass is likely to be used increasingly as a building material.

The material

Glass is an inorganic fusion product defined as a solidified liquid because a controlled cooling technique means that the material passes from the liquid to the solid state without crystallizing. The lack of a crystalline structure means that light penetrates the glass without diffusion and it seems transparent. Various chemicals can make glass, for example the oxides of silicon (Si), boron (B), germanium (Ge), phosphorous (P) and arsenic (As). As the main component of practically all glass products is silicon dioxide, it is usual to speak of silica glasses. Common building glass, so-called alkaline calcium silica glass, contains quartz sand, (SiO_2, 69–74 %), sodium (Na_2O, 12–16 %), calcium (CaO, 5–12 %) and some percentage of other materials that affect the properties or colour of the glass. Borosilicate glasses are made by adding boron (B_2O_3, 7–15 %) instead of calcium. They are used for fire safety, as their very low thermal expansion gives them a much greater resistance to temperature changes. In glass manufacture, the raw materials are first of all heated up until they are viscous, then processed and cooled slowly. During the cooling process, the high viscosity of the melt prevents the molecules from arranging themselves in a crystalline structure. This randomly solidified molecular condition is called "frozen".

Manufacturing processes

Glass is first and foremost a chance product of nature. It forms inside the earth because of the great heat and is spewed out when volcanoes erupt.
This natural product, like obsidian, was used by early civilizations as jewellery, for example, for arrowheads and for vessels. Archaeological finds in Egypt show that glass was being made there as many as 7,000 years ago. About 5,000 years ago Mesopotamian craftsmen discovered that silicon, calcium and metallic oxides could be made into a vitreous mass by applying great heat. Finally, the Phoenicians discovered glass-blowing in the first century BC. At about the same time, the Romans were able to make panes of glass up to 70 x 100 cm by the casting process. These techniques were lost with the fall of the Roman empire. Then the bottle-glass and moon-glass processes were developed in the 14th century. Cylinder blowing and drawing had been discovered as early as the 10th century, but by the 18th century things had advanced so far that flat glass panes from 180 x 230 cm to 210 x 130 cm could be made.
Mechanization of the cylinder blowing process meant that 190 x 1000 cm panes could be made from the early 20th century. The first continuous manufacturing process was the mechanical drawing process. This was patented almost simultaneously by Emile Fourcault in 1904 and Irwin W. Colburn around 1905. The meant that a continuous strip of glass 125 cm wide could be produced. Alistair Pilkington developed the float process in 1959. Here the molten glass is floated over a bath of molten tin, forming a glass strip with an almost plane surface 125 cm wide. Float plants produce up to 3,000 m^2 of flat glass with very high optical properties per hour.

Types of glass

Various types of glass are used in the building industry:

Float and window glass

Float glass is the most commonly used type of flat glass.
The maximum strip dimensions are 321 x 600 cm with a thickness of 2 to 19 mm. Greater lengths are possible, but significantly more expensive.
Thin glass (only 0.6 to 1.8 mm), window glass (1.8 to 3.8 mm) and thick glass (over 19 mm thick) are often made by the drawing process.
All the glass mentioned will be clear and distortion-free.

Cast and ornamental glass

Cast and ornamental glass is also produced as a continuous band. The glass melt is calibrated with rollers and stamped with a surface structure on one or two sides. A spot-welded wire mesh can be set in the soft glass during manufacture.
Cast and ornamental glass is translucent, because the light is diffused by the more or less strongly marked surface texture.

There are certain surface structures that were developed specially for diffusing daylight in a room.
The maximum dimensions and thicknesses differ according to design and manufacturer.

Polished wired glass
Polishing the surfaces produces a transparent wired glass with plane-parallel surfaces. Wired glass panes are used for optical reasons, but are not classed as safety glass.
The maximum dimensions of wired glass are 1.98 cm wide, 1.65 to 3.82 cm long and 6 to 10 mm thick.

Profiled glass
Cast glass strips can be supplied as louvred elements with textured surfaces (ill. 1). The webs reinforce the glass elements. The surfaces can be textured in various ways and provided with sun- or heat-protective coatings. These elements are available in standard widths of 22, 25, 32 and 50 cm, and 6 metres long. They are also made with wire inlays to make them more shatterproof.

Glass blocks
Glass blocks, formerly called glass bricks, consist of two shell-shaped glass sections that are reheated until they fuse at the points of contact to form a hollow glass body. They can be coloured in the body, and their surfaces can be smooth or textured. Glass block walls meet the requirements of fire prevention classes G60 and G120.
The standard dimensions are 15 x 15 cm to 30 x 30 cm, with a depth of 8–10 cm. Extra-large glass bricks of 43 x 43 cm were developed and manufactured specially for a Tokyo department store (page 9).

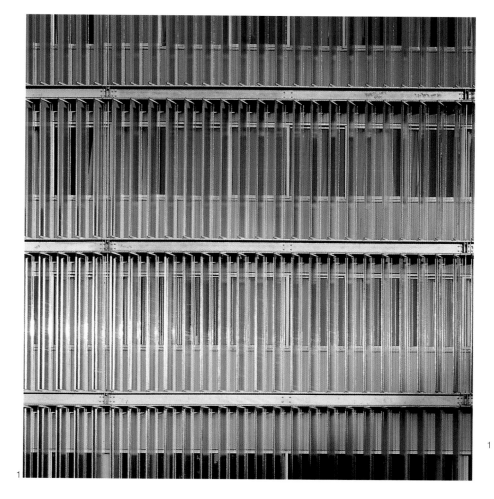

1   Institute building in Paris
    Wire reinforced figured glass elements as sun-breakers
    Architects: Jérôme Brunet & Eric Saunier, Paris

Qualities of glass

The structure and composition of glass affect its physical properties in relation to building to a considerable extent.

Optical properties

Glass is transparent because the molecules solidify without forming crystals; hence light can penetrate without being diffused. Glass allows the transmission of solar radiation with a wavelength between 315 and 2,500 nm, i.e. from the ultraviolet range of 315 to 380 nm via the visible range of 380 to 780 nm to the near IR range of 780 to 2,500 nm. The UV range under 315 nm and the long-wave IR range above 2,500 nm are completely absorbed. This impermeability to long-wave radiation explains glazing's greenhouse effect: solar radiation is transformed into heat in the interior, but cannot then escape as long-wave heat radiation.

Thermal properties

The decisive factor in terms of thermal loss through glass is its thermal conductivity. The thickness of a pane of glass has only a marginal effect in this respect, the degree of radiation can be controlled by coatings, and convection by the construction, e.g. insulated glazing.
Thermal expansion depends on the chemical composition of the glass. Alkaline calcium silicate glass have a thermal expansion of 9 $(10^{-6}K^{-1})$, and borosilicate glass 3–6 $(10\text{-}6K^{-1})$.

Physical characteristics

The terms reflection, absorption and transmission refer to the permeability of one or more panes of glass. They are expressed as a percentage of the total incident radiation (ill. 2). The light transmission value (τ value) defines the percentage of directly admitted, vertically incident light .

The total solar energy transmission value, the g-value, is the sum of directly transmitted vertical radiation and the secondary inward heat dissipation q by the glazing as a result of heat radiation, conductivity and convection.
The thermal transmission coefficient, the U-value, is the rate of heat loss through a 1 m² element per hour with a temperature difference of 1 Kelvin between the outside and inside air.

Bending strength

A high silicon dioxide content is important for hardness and bending strength, but also causes undesirable brittleness, which means that a pane of glass breaks when the limits of elastic distortion are minimally exceeded. While the theoretical tensile strength of glass is 104 N/mm², but practically is achieves a maximum of 30 to 60 N/mm² because of flaws and barely perceptible surface cracks.

Tempered glass

Low tensile strength can be increased by thermal or chemical tempering. This involves building up compressive stress in the surface, creating excess pressure in the cracks and flaws. So the load has to relieve the compressive prestress until it corresponds with the tensile strength of the glass (ills. 3,4).
For thermal tempering, the pane of glass is heated to approx. 680 °C and then has cold air blown at it abruptly so that the glass surface hardens immediately, while the core contracts more slowly. This creates tensile forces in the core area and compressive forces in the surface layer, which tempers the glass. A thermally tempered pane shatters into many crumbs without sharp edges, which minimizes the danger of injury. It is therefore known as tempered safety glass.
Microscopic particles of nickel sulphide can be trapped in the glass. These swell

on heating and can smash the pane very suddenly. For this reason, tempered safety glass is often subjected to a heat soak test, HST, before use. In the case of partially tempered glass, the cooling process is slower, so that the degree of prestress is somewhere between that of a normal, untreated pane and tempered safety glass. Partially tempered glass breaks into large pieces like a normal pane. Tempered safety glass has a bending strength of approx. 90 to 120 N/nm², and partially tempered glass approx. 40 to 75 N/nm². Chemical tempering is achieved by ion exchange on the surface of the glass. For this process, the glass is plunged into a hot salt melt. The sodium ions on the outside are exchanged with the large potassium ions, which creates compressive forces in a very thin surface layer.
Chemical tempering is used for thin panes like glass of cars, for example. The bending strength of chemically tempered glass is 200 N/nm². For this also see page 32.
Generally speaking, tempered glass cannot be further processed subsequently, e.g. cut or drilled.

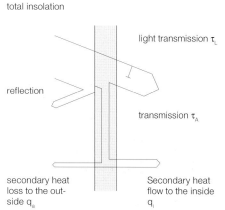

total insolation

light transmission τ_L

reflection

transmission τ_A

secondary heat loss to the outside q_a

Secondary heat flow to the inside q_i

2

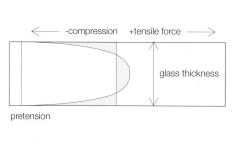

-compression   +tensile force

glass thickness

pretension

3

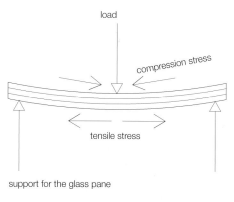

load

compression stress

tensile stress

support for the glass pane

4

2 Solar radiation through a pane of glass: reflection, absorption, transmission and overall energy transmission (g-value)
3 Internal stresses building up in toughened safety glass
4 Tension in the glass surface under load
5 Event venue and congress centre in San Sebastián, Spain
Material: curved laminated safety glass consisting of transparent figured glass and sand-blasted float glass
Architect: Rafael Moneo, Madrid

The glass facade

The radiation permeability of a pane of glass determines both the amount of heat and daylight entering a building and the amount leaving it.

In summer, the intention is to make the best use of daylight, but avoid undesirable heat gains.

In winter, however, heat gains are welcome, as they partially compensate for heat losses via the glass facade.

These partially conflicting requirements require a glass with changeable properties; this is still being developed.

Up to now, glazing has had to be complemented with additional protection against sunlight and heat. For glazing, glass is available with and without coating, and in combinations like laminated and insulating glass.

Glass panes

The properties of a pane of glass can be varied by changing the composition of the body of the glass and/or the pane's surface properties.

Float glass

Quartz sand, the most important raw material for glass manufacture, always contains minor impurities that cause discoloration. The slightly green cast in normal float glass comes from iron oxide (Fe_2O_3).

Typical values for a 4 mm thick float pane are a τ value of 0.9 and a g value of 0.87, but they vary according to the thickness of the glass (ill. 6).

White glass

Purer glass panes with a lower iron content, so-called "white glass", are created by chemically purifying the basic material or by using particularly pure raw materials. 4 mm thick "white glass" has a τ value of 0.92 and a g value of 0.9 (ill. 7).

Coloured glass

Adding metal oxides produces stronger coloration, with an associated reduction of light transmission. The colour range is currently restricted to green, blue, bronze and grey.

Green glass is produced by adding iron oxide and is the most common, 4 mm thick green glass has a τ value of 0.78 and a g value of 0.67.

Grey-tinted glass is made with nickel oxide, bronze glass with selenium; both are used to diminish glare.

Grey glass has a τ value of 0.54 and a g value of 0.67, bronze glass has a τ value of 0.55 and a g value of 0.65 (ill. 7).

Photosensitive glass

Photosensitive glass is a special development in colouring the body of the glass. Exposure to UV light and subsequent heat treatment create textures or patterns in the body of the glass. Corning Glass developed their Louverre ® product in 1983; its louvre-shaped structure is an aid to sunscreening.

Phototropic glass

Brown or grey phototropic glass is used to make spectacle lenses. It is a self-regulating product whose light permeability changes automatically with UV radiation. They have a large transmission range, for example, lenses can darken from 0.91 to 0.25 (ill.8).

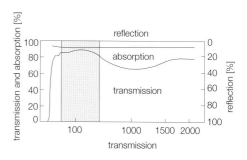

6   Diagram of spectral transmission in float glass

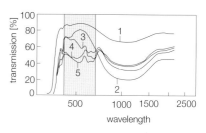

7   Diagram of spectral transmission in various tinted glasses
1 clear, 2 green, 3 blue, 4 bronze, 5 grey

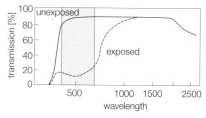

8   Diagram of spectral transmission in light-sensitive glass

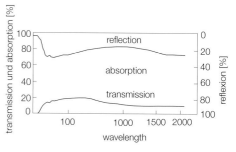

9   Diagram of spectral transmission in glass with a reflective coating

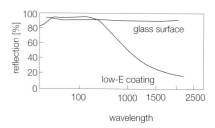

10 Diagram of spectral transmission in a low-E coated glass

Surface treatments

Subtractive and additive processes are other methods available for changing the properties of a pane of glass – so-called finishing. The subtractive processes work on the surface of the glass, e.g. by grinding, polishing or creating a matt surface. In the additive processes the surface of the glass is coated thinly or thickly, or laminated film is applied.

Grinding and polishing

Until the 1960s, especially clear and distortion-free glass was created by casting and rolling and then grinding and polishing on both sides. It was used for shop windows and mirrors, hence the name "mirror glass".

Matt surfaces

A roughened surface disperses incident daylight and thus reduces transparency. Matt surfaces can be created chemically or mechanically. All or part of the pane can be treated (ill. 11).
Etching is a chemical treatment with acid. The application time of the acid determines the degree of roughness or matt quality. Etched glass panes have been produced industrially since recently.
Sandblasting is a mechanical process for creating a matt surface. The depth is governed by the length of time the process lasts.

Thin coatings

Thin layers of precious metal and/or metal oxides are applied to clear or coloured glass to influence light transmission. Thin coatings are applied either online, i.e. immediately after the glass is made, in the float plant, or offline, as a later process.
Online coatings are created using a chemical reaction, the so-called CD (chemical deposition) process. The coating material is applied to the warm float glass strip either in liquid or vapour form, or in solid form, as powder. The chemical reaction produces a hard layer that resists wear and chemical effects. Hard-coated glass can be used as single glazing.
Offline, the glass is coated using the dipping or the vacuum process.
In the dipping process, the glass is dipped in sol-gel solutions and subsequently fired. This process coats both surfaces.
In the vacuum process, the so-called TVD process, the coating material is vaporized in multi-chamber high-vacuum plant and by cathode sputtering and condensed on to the glass surface. The coating is usually built up of individual layers that can be applied in any thickness required and very evenly.
The vacuum process usually creates so-called soft coatings.
Light transmission can be flexibly adjusted by varying the structure and thickness of the coating. But these coatings tend to be soft and sensitive to aggressive air pollution and mechanical pressure. For this reason they have to be protected by inclusion in a double- or triple-glazing system.

Heat insulation and sunscreening

Layers of called low-E (emission) coatings are used for thermal insulation. They reduce the emissive quality of the glass surface, and thus its radiant heat loss. Conductive metal layers based on gold, silver or copper are used for this. Silver-based coatings have become accepted recently because they offer maximum colour neutrality with the greatest possible light transmission.
For sunscreening, reflective silver, gold or metal oxide coatings are used, mainly based on nickel-chrome, stainless steel or other alloys. These metallic coatings increase reflection, thus reducing transmission and radiation as a whole. They can be applied to clear or tinted glass.
τ values of 0.2 to 0.75 and g-values of 0.1 to 0.65 are usual for sunscreening glass (ill. 9).
The layer structure can also include selective properties guaranteeing high transmission in the visible range and at the same time low infrared transmission.

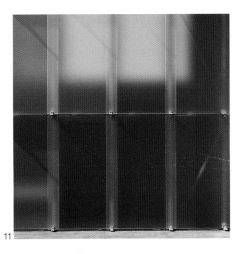

11

11 Kunsthaus Bregenz
Panes of toughened safety glass (2x10 mm white glass, 4xPVB film), etched on one side
Architect: Peter Zumthor, Haldenstein/CH

12

12 Glass sculpture "Dichroic Light Field", New York
   Artist: James Carpenter, New York
13 Herz-Jesu church in Munich
   Portal glazing
   "Float glass painting", raised, transparent fritted
   coating on insulation glass
   Artist: Alexander Beleschenko, Swansea/UK
   Architects: Allmann Sattler Wappner, Munich
14 Indoor swimming-pool in Bad Elster
   Overhead sunscreen louvres in laminated safety
   glass,
   screen colour printing
   Architects: Behnisch und Partner Stuttgart
   Günter Behnisch, Manfred Sabatke
   Façade consultancy: Ingenieurbüro Brecht,
   Stuttgart
15 "Barbarossa Center" in Cologne
   Light band with monochrome blue light-emitting
   diodes
   Architects: Busman & Haberer GmbH, Cologne
   Light planning: ag Licht, Bonn

Special coatings

Optical coatings are appropriate for special uses in medicine, and in lighting and industry.

- Cold-mirror coatings work like "reverse" low-E systems by reflecting the visible wavelengths and transmitting the IR range. They are used in reflectors for dichroic lamps or projectors.

- Anti-reflection coatings reduce the reflection from glass panes from about 8 % to about 1 %, thus increasing light transmission. They are used for glazing showcases or advertising panels (Amiran®, Mirogas®, Luxar®).

- Dichroic coatings cause a shift from transmission to reflection in the visible light range. This breaks the light down into complementary colours.
  Glass of this kind is used for special filters in measuring and lab technology. The architect and glass specialist James Carpenter used dichroic glass for a lot of his art-in-building projects (ill. 12).

- Electroconductive coatings are layers and layer systems based on indium oxide (ITO) and silver. They form electrically conductive coatings that can be used for EC (electrochrome) coating, for example.

- Dirt resistant coatings stop glass from getting dirty as a result of environmental influences and make it easier to clean. This effect is produced by changing the wettability properties of the glass surface. Hydrophobic coatings make the water form droplets that run off very quickly Hydrophilic coatings make the water spread out and form a transparent film.

Thick coatings

Thick coatings comprise protective and enamel coatings and laminated plastic films. They are almost all produced offline.

- Protective coatings
  Protective lacquer is applied to protect the thin layer of silver on a mirror. It is produced by fogging: the mirror is drawn through a fog created by a slit nozzle.

- Enamel coatings
  Enamelled glass is given a ceramic coating that is resistant to wear and tear and to weathering. The enamel coating is created by applying a frit of finely ground glass with various additives and colour pigments to the glass and then firing it on. Enamelling can cover the entire pane, or be applied in printed patterns. Roller application covers the whole surface: the layer of colour is applied with a pressure roller. A dosing roller controls the thickness of the layer. Patterns of dots, lines and bars are created by a screen-printing process, evenly or with flow-out. The pattern is transferred to the pane by a stencil, and each layer is allowed to dry separately if there is more than one colour (ills. 13 and 14). Enamelled patterns can be made into light panels. Here artificial light is from light-emitting diodes is introduced from the edge of the pane, visible through the printed enamel. Light-emitting diodes make all kinds of colour grading possible (ill. 15). Conductor tracks with conductor gel are used for car panes with integrated heating or aerials, for example.

Laminated plastic film

Plastic film, which bonds the splinters together, can be applied to glass to minimize the danger of injury when a pane of glass breaks. There are also plastic films on the market offering thermal insulation and sunscreening. These products have not yet become accepted in Europe. The film is applied to the glass from a feeder roll during manufacture.

13

14

15

Multi-layered glass

Multi-layered construction makes it possible to combine glass panes with and without coating and with intermediate spaces of varying depths. This make it possible to build in various thermal insulation and sunscreening measures.

Laminated glass

Laminated glass is made up of one or more panes with an intermediate layer. Laminated glass with no safety features can be used for sound insulation or decorative purposes. Cast resins and various kinds of plastic membrane can be used as the intermediate layer: transparent, tinted and patterned, UV absorbent and IR reflective film, film with wire inlays for security, alarm or heating purposes. Cast resin is poured between the panes and then fixed by UV radiation or chemical treatment. Plastic film is laminated between the panes. It is also possible to buy laminated glass with intermediate metal mesh layers (OkaTech®), veneered wood (Chrisunid®), and glass mat (Thermolux®).

It is even possible to fix light-emitting diodes between the layers, activated by a power supply from a transparent conductive coating (Power-Glass®).

Laminated safety glass

The commonest use of laminated glass is laminated safety glass, which is made with an intermediate layer of polyvinyl-butyral (PVB) film. If the glass breaks, the splinters stick to the elastic PVB film, considerably reducing the risk of injury. Another advantage of laminated safety glass is that unlike float and tempered safety glass it does not shatter into fragments, but can hold back people or objects that cannon into it where necessary. Typical uses of laminated safety glass are for overhead glazing and glass used to prevent falling, like glass parapets or floor-to-ceiling glazing (ills. 11, 14).

Laminated safety glass is made by placing PVB film with a thickness of 0.38 or 0.76 mm between the glass panes and pressing them together in an autoclave with heat and low pressure. Tempered safety glass or partially tempered glass are often used for laminated safety glass, as they are stronger than normal float glass.

Partially tempered glass has the advantage over tempered safety glass when it breaks that it gives better residual structural stability because larger pieces stick to the intermediate layer.

16 Walkway link in Rotterdam
    Laminated glass floor slabs (2 x15 mm) on two glass supports
    Architects: Dirk Jan Postel, Kraaijvanger • Urbis, Rotterdam
    Structural engineering: Rob Nisse, ABT Velp
17 Examples of different compositions for fire-retardant glass
18 Bullet-resistant glass
19 Fire retardant glass, demonstration of thermal insulation using Pilkington Pyrostop®

16

Glass that can be stepped or walked on
Laminated glass is also used for glazing that can be stepped or walked on, to ensure that no one will fall (ill. 16).
Glass that can be stepped on is accessible only to cleaning and service personnel. Concentrated loads are taken into account as well as distributed loads when dimensions are calculated.
Glazing that can be walked on is accessible to all and is thus dimensioned like a normal floor slab. It also has to be possible to carry heavy objects across them. A wear-pane is often provided as a protective layer on load-bearing glass. It will have a matt surface or rough enamel printing to avoid slippage.

Laminated glass resistant to thrown objects, breakage and bullets
Various safety requirements can be met by combining different thicknesses of glass and film (ill. 18).
The glass can be resistant to:

• thrown objects
• breakage
• bullets
• explosives.

Laminated safety glass combinations of this kind can be up to 10 cm thick (SSG-Contracrime®).

Laminated glass for sound insulation
Sound waves can be damped by soft and sound-absorbent intermediate layers. Here the vibrations in the two glass panes are neutralized.
Most laminated glass for sound insulation is made with a cast resin layer about 1 mm thick (Ipaphon®). Plastic film for sound insulation has also appeared on the market recently (Trosifol-Sound-Control®).

Fire-retardant laminated glass
Fire-retardant glass is used as a preventive measure intended to restrict or at least delay fire from spreading in a building. Fire-retardant requirements vary between integrity for 30 minutes to 90 minutes thermal insulation, dependent on the structure and thickness of the laminated glass. Layers of water-glass 1 to 2 mm thick or water-glass gels 10mm and more thick are used as intermediate layers. When water-glass layers are used a fluid water-salt solution is poured on to the base pane, dried and then laminated on to the covering pane. The number of

layers can be increased to meet the appropriate requirements.
Fire-retardant glass using water-gels is made by the cast resin process. The water solution is poured in fluid form and then treated. The fire-retardant time afforded is calculated from the thickness. Fire-retardant glass is approved as a unit with the frame construction and the sealing system and thus only be used as a complete component (ill. 17, 19).

17: Examples of various fire-retardant glass compositions

Contraflam®		F30	F90
Basis:	Soda-lime glass, tempered (Sekurit)		
Structure:	A gel containing a water-soluble salt solution is sandwiched between two panes		
Function:	The sandwiched water evaporates, the gel becomes opaque and forms a heat shield		
Service life:	The gel layer is enlarged to increase the high fire resistance life	Single glass: 25 mm Insulating glass: > 36 mm	Single glass: 60 mm Insulating glass: > 71 mm
Promaglas®		F30	F90
Basis:	Soda-lime glass		
Structure:	Several panes of glass of different thickness with alkali silicate layers between the panes		
Function:	Intermediate layers foam to produce a tough, solid mass		
Service life:	The number of panes and layers is increased to achieve the high level of fire resistance	Single glass: 17 mm Insulating glass: > 35 mm	Single glass: 43 mm Insulating glass: > 61 mm
Pyrostop®		F30	F90
Basis:	Soda-lime glass (Optifloat)		
Structure:	Several panes of glass with alkali silicate layers between the panes		
Function:	Intermediate layers foam to produce a tough, solid mass		
Service life:	The number of panes and layers is increased to achieve the high level of fire resistance	Single glass: 15 mm Insulating glass: > 32 mm	Single glass: 50 mm Insulating glass: > 56 mm
Glass blocks		F60	
Basis:	DIN 18175 glass blocks		
Structure:	double-layer		
Function:	Compact glass blocks with tie bar	Overall thickness 200 mm	

18

19

Laminated glass with functional layers
Functional layers that diffract light or serve the needs of sunscreening and thermal protection are another promising development.

• Incidence angle-selective layers
Transparent plastic films are available that transmit light only at a certain angle of incidence, becoming non-transparent in the process. In principle they consist of a microscopic louvre structure created in the film by photo-polymerization.

• Layers with holographic-optical elements
Holographic-optical elements (HOE) make various light deflection variants possible through diffraction, rather like mirrors, lenses, prisms and other optical elements. They are records of interference patterns created by laser light on high-resolution photographic film. The light is deflected only for the set angle of incidence, so the holograms have to track the incident light.
In architecture, holographic-optical elements are used for light deflection, sunscreening and displays. In displays the light decomposition creates spectral colours of extraordinary luminosity (ill. 20, 21).

• Layers with photovoltaic modules
Laminated glass with photovoltaic (PV) modules can convert solar energy into electricity and provide sunscreening at the same time (ill. 22). PV modules usually consist of silicon solar cells; a distinction must be made between mono- and polycrystalline, and also amorphous, solar cells. Monocrystalline solar cells are opaque, range in colour from blue or dark grey to black, and are 14–16 % efficient. They are made by an elaborate and therefore expensive process from silicon crystal. Polycrystalline solar cells are usually blue and opaque. They are more affordable because they are derived from cast silicon blocks, but they are only 11–13 % effective. Crystalline solar cells are manufactured as panes 0.4 mm thick and with dimensions of 10 x 10 to 15 x 15 cm. They are then assembled as modules and bedded into the cavity in the laminated glass with cast resin. Different colours like gold, brown, green magenta, purple etc. have been available for some time now. As they are not dark, they absorb less solar energy and are less effective.
Amorphous solar cells are non-crystalline. They are manufactured by the thin-film process and are 8 to 10 % effective. They are available as opaque or semi-transparent modules. In the case of the semi-transparent modules, parts of the layers are removed by laser separation so that transparent strips are created between the active areas (Asi-Glas®). Amorphous solar cells made of other materials like CdTe and CuInSe$_2$ are still being developed; they are intended to be 10 to 12 % efficient.

20

20 Shopping centre in Lille, arcade facade
    Material: insulating glass with holographic film and images
    Architect: Jean Nouvel, Paris
21 Further education academy in Herne
    Holographic elements in the overhead glazing
    Architects: Jourda et Perraudin, Lyon (competition, planning)
    Hegger Hegger Schleiff, Kassel (planning)
22 Further education academy in Herne
    Photovoltaic modules in the facade
23 Layers with liquid crystals
    Glazing for a seminar room, with and without a view through
24 Schematic diagram of micro-encapsulated liquid crystals
25 Structure of a thermotropic layer
26 Structure of electrochromic layers according to Professor Claes G. Grandquist, Uppsala

21

22

Optically variable systems
Various systems are currently being investigated in which radiation transmission can be controlled automatically or by mechanical means. Only prototypes have been developed so far, industrial production has not yet started.
The layers alter energy transmission when there is a change of temperature. Electro-optical layers containing liquid crystals or electrochromic materials change when an electric charge is applied.

- *Thermotropic and thermochromic layers*
  Thermotropic layers respond to the whole range of solar radiation. As the temperature rises, they pass from being clear and transparent into an opaque state in which they diffract the light. The basic material is a combination of two different polymers with different refractive indices, such as water and a plastic (hydrogel) or two different kinds of plastic (polymer blend). At low temperatures, the material is homogeneous and transparent. When heated, the polymers change their configuration, which results in the diffraction of light. The change is reversible (ill. 25). When exposed to heat, thermochromic layers undergo a change in their transmission properties, particularly in the nearer IR range. They are thus suitable for use as low-E coatings to reduce thermal loss. It is not yet possible to predict what development might bring.

- Layers with liquid crystals
  Liquid crystal systems work because the needle-shaped liquid crystals can be aligned electrically. This makes the system translucent, and it remains in this state for as long as the current is applied. The light-transmitting values vary from 0.7 in an opaque state to 0.73 in a transparent state. The layers of film are approx. 0.3 mm thick and have a maximum area of 1 x 2.8 m. LC films can presently be used without difficulty at temperatures from -40 °C to 40 °C. So liquid crystal systems are usually used indoors for temporary sight protection. LC displays are a special feature. The glass is divided into pixels that can be switched on in various combinations: as letters, numbers or images. LC displays are used for information panels and can also be made up as video tapes (ills. 22, 23).

- Electrochromic layers
  These systems exploit the properties of certain materials to absorb or shed ions, thus modifying their transmission throughout the transmission range. In principle, they work like an accumulator: an ion storage layer, an ion conductor and an electrochromic material are sandwiched between two substrates – glass or plastic – with transparent electrodes. When an electrical charge is applied a chemical reaction occurs and the ions move backwards and forwards. The layers remain charged for some time, and so electricity is needed only during the ion exchange. The most commonly used substance is tungsten oxide (WO_3) because it permits the maximum variation of intensity between transparent and dark blue in the visible range. It is possible to create other colours or colour changes, however. Electrochromic systems can are continuously variable between a transparent and an absorbing state (ill. 26). They are thus suitable for sunscreening or protection against glare, both in buildings and for glazing in aircraft and road and rail vehicles. Insulating glass with EC panes (E-Control®) can change light transmission from 0.5 in the clear state to 0.15 in the darkened state. Thus the g-value can be adjusted between 0.4 and 0.14.

- Gas-chromatic systems
  Gas-chromatic systems were developed from the electrochromic principle. Here the colour change is caused by a catalytic reaction between the coating and a gas mixture. The system is constructed like insulating glass; in this case, the gap is filled with a gas mixture. The layers have a coating made up of tungsten oxide (WO_3) and a covering layer of platinum. The thickness of the layer and the gas concentration make it possible to achieve almost any desired level of transmission. The first prototypes were introduced as early as 1998.

23

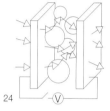
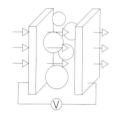

24

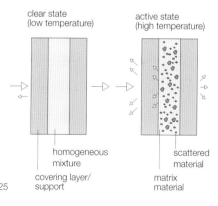

clear state (low temperature)   active state (high temperature)

homogeneous mixture   scattered material
covering layer/ support   matrix material

25

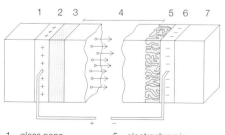

1   2   3   4   5   6   7

1 glass pane
2 transparent electrode
3 ion storage layer
4 ion conductor

5 electrochromic material
6 transparent electrode
7 glass pane

26

27

Insulated glazing

Insulating glass is made up of two or more glass panes connected by one or more spacers so that are shear- and gastight. This creates a dry air-filled gap that works as a heat buffer.
All the glass types used so far can be used for insulating glass.

Heat insulation
Heat loss from a monolithic pane of glass of 6 W/m^{2}K can be reduced to approx. 3 W/m^{2}K by the use of insulating glass. Heat loss occurs in four ways with insulating glass: radiation between the opposing glass panes, convection in the gap, heat conduction via the filling or via the peripheral connection. Various measures can reduce this heat loss (ill. 29).
Radiation exchange between the opposing glass panes can be reduced with a thermal insulation coating. An untreated glass surface has an emissivity of about 96 %, but a surface with a thermal insulation coating has an emissivity of 3–12 %. This reduced the U-value of air-filled insulating glass from 3W/m^{2}K to under 2 W/m^{2}K. Convection and heat conduction in the air gap are already low, but can be further reduced by using inert gases like argon and/or krypton. Inert gases also reduce convection.
With argon filling the U-value is 1.1 W/m^{2}K, with a krypton filling 0.8 W/m^{2}K. The ultimate choice criteria are financial.
Heat conduction via the usual aluminium spacers can be considerably reduced by the used of peripheral connection systems in stainless steel plastic with a metal inlay or thermoplastic material. The U-value can be further reduced by fitting a third pane into the gap, by adding a stretched membrane, or by creating a vacuum in the gap.
Triple glazing with two low-E coatings and an argon filling achieves a U-value of

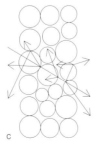

28 a   b   c   d

27 School in Collombey, CH
Figured glass elements filled with translucent cellulose mesh
Architects:
Olivier Galletti et Claude Matter, Lausanne
Facade consultancy: Acomet SA, Collombey
28 Geometrical ordering principles for transparent heat insulation
a structures parallel with the glass;
b structures vertical to the glass;
c cellular structures;
d quasi homogeneous structures
29 Heat transfer in insulating glass
30 Various types of insulating glass:
a triple insulating glass with two low-E coatings
b insulating glass with membranes
31 School in Collombey, CH
Architects:
Olivier Galletti et Claude Matter, Lausanne
Facade consultancy: Acomet SA, Collombey

0.7 W/m²K, and with krypton filling a
U-value of 0.5 W/m²K.
Fitting a low-emission coated membrane
avoids the weight and thickness of a third
glass pane (ill. 30).
Evacuating the gap can further reduce
heat conduction by the enclosed gas. But
it does create other problems in respect
of seal tightness and thermal separation.
Early vacuum glazing prototypes achieve
a U-value of 0.6 W/m²K, but it will still take
some time before full industrial production
is possible.

Fillings with thermal insulation properties
Transparent heat insulators make it possible to reduce heat loss and at the same
time gain heat from the incident sunlight
(ills. 27, 31).
Transparent and translucent materials like
glass, acrylic glass (PMMA), polycarbonate (PC) and quartz foam are used, in
layers of varying thickness and structure.
They are protected from the weather and
mechanical damage by being built in
between two panes (ills. 28, 30).
They are classified according to four geometrical arrangements of the structure:

· Structures parallel with the external
glass like double or triple glazing or
membrane systems reduce heat loss
but cause higher reflection loss.

· Structures that are vertical to the external glass consist of honeycombs or
capillary elements that divide the gaps
into small air cells.
This arrangement reduces reflection
loss, as the incident radiation is
directed inside by multiple reflection on
the parallel walls.
Honeycomb structures look like multi-
stay bridges made of transparent polycarbonate. Capillary structures are
assembled from large numbers of small
glass or plastic tubes.
A 100 mm thick capillary sheet made of
small polycarbonate tubes achieves a
U-value of 0.89 W/m²K and a τ-value of
0.69 (Oka-Lux®).
Capillary structures made up of
100 mm long small glass tubes have
achieved U-values around 1 W/m²K.

· Cellular structures result from combining parallel and vertical structures, like
acrylic foam, for example.

· Quasi-homogeneous structures such as
aerogels are microscopically cellular.
The manufacture of aerogel sheets is
very elaborate and thus expensive.
Aerogel granules are much more reasonably priced; they are packed loose
into the gap between the panes. A 16
mm granular filling (Basogel®) achieves
a U-value of less than 0.8 W/m²K, a
τ-value of 0.41 and a gdiff-value of 0.52
(ill. 33).

Comparing the four thermal insulation
groups shows that insulating glass and
plastic membrane systems are best in
areas where transparency is required for
visibility reasons. They also ensure low
U-values.
Other structures are more or less light-
diffusing and thus suitable for roof-light
glazing.
In summer, transparent heat insulation
needs sunscreening to prevent the
spaces from heating up.

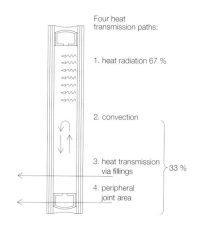

29

a

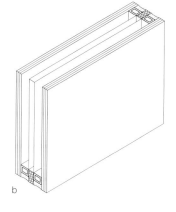

30   b

31

32

33

32 Various types of transparent heat insulation
33 Aerogels (Basogel®)
34 Development centre in Ingolstadt
   Insulating glass panes with integral, electronically
   controlled shading louvres
   Architects: Fink + Jocher, Munich
35 Light-deflecting glass
   a vertical deflection through special profiling on
   the inside, vertical section
   1 glass, 2 acrylic elements in the airspace, 3 cast
   glass
   b vertical deflection through special profiling on
   the inside, horizontal section
   c light deflecting system, vertical section
   solar incidence pattern: above: summer sun,
   below: winter sun

Sunscreening
The use of tinted or reflective insulating glass is not sufficient to meet today's sunscreening requirements of g-values less that 0.15.
Enamelled insulating glass with printed patterns is also not enough to meet these requirements. They are used for design purposes and have to be complemented by other sunscreening measures. The g-value derives from the ration of transparent to opaque areas and their absorption.

Fillings with sunscreening properties
The intermediate space between the layers of glazing can also be used to accommodate sunscreening devices, e.g membranes, woven materials and louvres. They are protected against soiling and the weather, thus reducing cleaning and maintenance costs. There are systems on the market using timber grids (OkaWood®), metal meshes (OkaTech®) and metal honeycombs. Systems that can be regulated, like blinds or louvres, can also be included in the cavity space, along with the necessary electric motors. Blinds are fitted with reflective film (Agero®) or with coloured polyster mesh (Trisolux®).
Louvres are adjusted magnetically or electrically (Luxaclair®, Velthec®).

Fillings with light-deflecting properties
Light deflection systems are based on optical properties such as reflection, transmission and refraction. They screen out direct sunlight but admit diffuse daylight into the interior.

• Light-grid devices consist of highly reflective plastic louvres that form rows of narrow light-shafts. The shape of the louvres and the orientation of the openings allow diffused daylight into the interior while reflecting direct sunlight. Depending on the composition of the glass elements, g-values of around 0.2 can be achieved.

• Daylight-control systems using prismatic sheets of acrylic glass (PMMA) are based on complete reflection of sunlight falling on the edges of the prisms. Since this area is very small, the prismatic sheet has to be moved to track the movement of the sun. Its scope can be considerably increased by coating one prism edge with pure aluminium. Light deflection further inside the space is achieved with additional light-deflecting prisms.

• In the Lumitop® light deflection system, slightly curved acrylic sections are built into the cavity. This rounded form allows complete reflection of a wide range of incident light, both horizontally and vertically.

• OkaSolar® reflective elements are built in and offer sunscreening or light deflection according to the elevation of the sun. The system consists of specially shaped mirror elements whose profile is designed to relate to the different angles of incidence of sunlight. Steeply incident summer light is reflected outwards, while deep-incident winter light is admitted and deflected into the space. The louvres are installed at the optimum angle for the required use (ill. 35c). The g-value varies according to the sun's elevation from 0.22 to 0.51, the τ-value from 0.03 to 0.51 (OkaSolar® type 55/15).

34

Looking ahead

A look at current architecture shows the great variety of innovative glass products available for exterior and interior use. Here it is not just transparency or design advantages that are crucial, but developments in building physics as well. But there are technical limitations affecting manufacture and finishing formats that can differ greatly from producer to producer.

The most recent progress in building physics has meant that using insulating glass can achieve very low heat loss, and sometimes passive energy gains even lead to heat gains.

In our latitudes, adaptable summer heat protection is an important topic. Selective coatings have been developed, but the aim is better adaptation to the changing weather conditions. This means that glazing with changeable properties is needed.

Early products exist as prototypes, but more progress is needed to do justice to technical and economic aspects. Development potential in the field of glass technology is far from being exhausted, so it seems likely that glass as a building material will continue to impress us with technical innovations in the future.

35

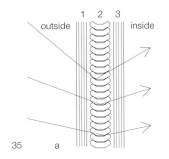

a

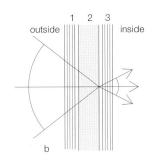

b

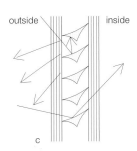

c

**Structural glass –
Research and innovations**

Glass technology has definitely not stopped developing. Glass can now be used as a load-bearing element, rather than simply to fill in support structures made of other materials. Extensive research is being conducted on this subject and cannot be covered exhaustively within the scope of this book. Four projects that mainly addressed the material aspects of structural building with glass stand as example for glass's development potential in this field as well.

· Compound glass tubes as a structural element in glass skeleton construction

· Glass shells bonded to form a load-bearing glass dome without additional support structure

· Reinforced laminated glass with metal mesh or fibre between the panes

· Composite structure using fibre-reinforced plastic elements with glass panes

1

Glass skeleton construction with compound glass tubes

Joachim Achenbach

Some innovative buildings have emerged in recent years using glass as a structural building material. In all the projects realized to date, the load-bearing structures have consisted mainly of laminated glass panes using tempered or partially tempered plate glass. Other materials, like for example stone, wood or steel have been used to manufacture rod-shaped as well as flat building materials from time immemorial, but structural work with glass remains trapped in "building with panes and walls" or more precisely, transparent massive construction (ill.1).

Hence compound glass tubes expand the architectural repertory, as they can be used to realize genuine glass skeleton buildings. Compound glass tubes, in their round, axially symmetric form, for example, have ideal statical properties.

Material properties
Borosilicate glass, which is used as a rule for drawing glass tubes (DURAN®), has outstanding properties: transparency, colour neutrality, chemical resistance, thermal shock resistance and the high level of homogeneity essential for coping with mechanical stress. An additional feature is that glass tube elements can be manufactured with relatively low tolerances in respect of cross-section (e.g. roundness), wall thickness, longitudinal curvature etc. [4].

Such precision is needed for further processing to make structurally viable building components and for controlled load introduction.

Manufacturing glass tubes
Glass tube manufacture could not be simpler. Liquid glass is gravity-fed over a revolving pipe, which has air blown through it. The glass tube produced in this way is picked up by a drawing machine, drawn out and cooled on a conveyor belt under controlled conditions. For diameters of 50 to 100 mm the drawing proceeds horizontally (Vello drawing process). For smaller diameters, glass tubes can theoretically be drawn to any length [3]. For diameters of over 100 to 150 mm it is not possible to switch from the vertical to the horizontal. For this reason, the glass is drawn vertically in a drawing pit (downward drawing process). The maximum manufacturing length for such glass tubes is currently approx. 4,100 mm.

For tube diameters of between 155 and 270 mm the length is restricted to 2,500 mm because of the greater dead weight and increased difficulty in handling due to the not entirely rigid, red-hot body of glass; the maximum length for diameters up to 450 mm is 2,000 mm. The walls can be from 1.8 to 9 mm with tube diameters of 50 to 270 mm. Above this, wall thicknesses of up to 10 mm are possible.

Manufacturing laminated glass tubes
Laminated glass tubes can be manufactured only by dividing the outer glass tube into half-shells longitudinally. If the laminated glass tubes are over 1,500 mm long, the half-shells also have to be divided transversely. The "manufacturing joins", which are scarcely visible to the naked eye, also help to dissipate secondary bending forces inside the multi-layered structure when the temperature changes. It is only in this way that adequately durable laminated tube construction elements can be created for the building industry.

Of all the theoretically possible ways of making laminated glass tubes, an innovative modification of the autoclave process has turned out to be the most reliable. After the individual parts have been placed in position, the glass tube and the coaxial tube half-shells are bonded practically permanently under heat and pressure, using toughened, transparent polymer film (polyvinylbuteral resin or polyurethane). Bonding the two glass tubes, with the inner tube bearing the load and the outer tube protecting it, has the effect of holding splinters together in cases of breakage, and also stabilizes the shape, one of many factors involved in the particular safety level of laminated glass tubes. This process also ensures that the positive material properties of glass tubes are retained in laminated tubes to the greatest possible extent, which means that the requirements made of structural glass tube elements in the building industry can be met (ill. 2).

Transfer of force by the end component
But the high efficiency of a laminated glass tube is not determined by the composite effect in the normal cross-section of the element. It is only when combined with a custom-built glass tube end section with specific characteristics that the enormous potential of laminated glass tubes as a system building component can be fully realized (ill. 3).

End components for structural glass tubes are made up from three main groups:

A base plate, a centring piece that concentrates the forces and an interface bolt,

1 "Laminata" detached house, Leerdam
Walls made of vertical float glass sheets bonded with adhesive. Architect: Kruunenberg Van der Erve Architecten, Amsterdam

27

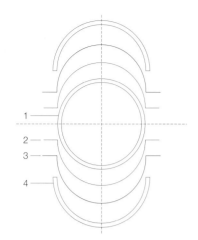

2

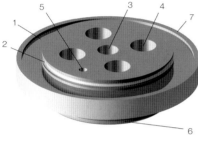

3

preferably articulated, for attachment to the building or to other components. Crucial function features are the material properties and shape of the base plate, special techniques for processing the end of the tube and the direct mounting of the end of the glass tube on the base plate, which will deviate from the principles of flat glass mounting. If all these requirements are met, laminated glass tubes can transfer comparable forces to steel tubes.

Bearing capacity
Glass tube elements can sustain loads of at least 400 N/mm² of axial pressure. Serial tests have shown no failures with such loads. These do not occur until the stresses are much greater, sometimes only when approaching pressure loads of 1,000 N/mm². This makes for an admissible compression stress of 60 N/mm² as a typical value with even the most conservative of approaches, and this already has a multiple safety factor built in. The maximum admissible tension gives a value of 7 Nmm². Thus for example a glass tube with an external diameter of 200 mm and walls 9 mm thick (contact area 5,400 mm²) can take loads of approx. 33 tons. This corresponds with the load borne in the

case of a flat roof with a support grid of 10 x 10 m (catchment area 100 m²) and an area weight of 2.5 kNm², plus 0.75 kNm² snow load (total 3.25 kNm²) [1].

Breaking
Unlike plate glass, which can take only minor pressure loads, very large compressive forces can be transferred by glass tubes before a component fails. Tubular geometry provides a statically optimal profile with economical use of materials. A borosilicate glass tube (DURAN®) with an external diameter of 150 mm, walls 5 mm thick and 4,100 mm long (high) is mounted vertically at load case 2 (breaking length = 1L) and loaded axially. The test item breaks at a load of 221,678.0 N. The critical load applied is 97.3 N/mm².
If cut open and unrolled, the tube produces a flat glass pane approx. 471 mm wide, with walls 5 mm thick and 4,100 mm high. If a pane of this kind – given identical mounting – is also loaded axially, this will break at a force of only 175 N and a critical load of 0.077 N/mm². The compressive force from own mass is 210 N in each test. This example shows that a large pane of flat glass, placed ver-

2 Laminated glass tube scheme
   1 Internal load-bearing tube (3.3 borosilicate glass)
   2 Polyvinylbuteral resin and/or polyurethane film
   3 more layers of film where necessary
   4 external protective tube made up of half-shells
3 Base-plate/endpiece scheme
   1 glass contact area, 2 docking flange for O-ring
   3 central channel, 4 molecular sieve points
   5 capillary channel (for possible pressure compensation)
   6 central thread, 7 peripheral lip
4 Detail of glass bridge
5 Experimental glass bridge structure with students
6 Tower Place, London, atrium facade
   Architect: Norman Foster and Partners, London
   Concept „Glass Tube Field":
   James Carpenter Design Associates, London
   Structural engineering: Ove Arup, London
   Steel/glass construction: Waagner Biro, Vienna
   Laminated glass tubes: Schott Rohrglas, Mitterteich
7 Laminated glass tube, Schott Rohrglas, Mitterteich
8 System component set

Suggested literature:

[1] Achenbach, Joachim; Behling, Stefan; Doenitz, Fritz-Dieter; Jung, Herbert:
    "Konstruktive Elemente aus Glasrohrprofilen".
    In: Glas Architektur und Technik, issue 5/2002, pp 5 – 10, Stuttgart: DVA
[2] Achenbach, Joachim; Jung, Herbert:
    "Konstruktive Elemente aus Glasrohrprofilen in Tragstrukturen – Systementwicklung, Herstellung und Anwendung" and "Leistungsvermögen von Verbundglasrohren". In: GlasKon 2003 pp. 29–34. Messe München GmbH(4)
[3] Doenitz, Fritz-Dieter; Achenbach, Joachim:
    "Glasrohre und Glasprofile" and „Möglichkeiten der Anwendung in der Architektur"
    In: GlasKon '99. Messe München GmbH
[4] Schott Rohrglas GmbH (publ.):
    Glasrohrprofile aus Borosilicatglas 3.3 DURAN® nach DIN ISO 3585 u. ASTM E 438 Typ 1, Klasse A. Company brochure

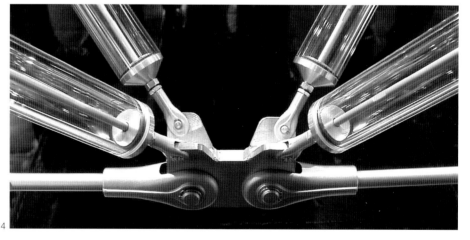

4

5

tically, cannot actually bear more than its own weight, while a glass tube using the same materials is considerably more efficient and very well suited to transferring forces [2].

Safety
Load-bearing and safety tests at the Fachhochschule in Munich and the Staatliche Materialprüfanstalt at the University of Stuttgart have confirmed that laminated glass tubes remain extremely efficient even when badly damaged, and display a residual structural stability that exceeded all expectations. Thus for example, laminated tubes that were penetrated by steel bars a number of times (bullet simulation) and struck over a dozen times by a 10 kg steel ball from a height of 1 metre (pendulum impact test) can still sustain their designated load. Residual structural stability is guaranteed despite all this.

Compatibility and integration capacity
One important aspect of the use and design possibilities of laminated glass tube is their compatibility with other building construction components that are already available, like for example end, connection and node components made by Mero or Rhodan-Dorma. Components of this kind can be a suitable alternative to project-specific serial production, according to the particular project. Integrating other technical systems and functions appeals precisely because of the transparency of the building material and opens up other development possibilities, for example lighting built into the end component, functional items like LED light sources, printing or coatings, possibly light-diffusing, that can be built into the lamination.

Possible design and usage
Laminated glass tubes with a circular cross-section are available in various exterior diameters (e.g. 100 mm, 165 mm, 183 mm), and up to a length of 4,100 mm, which means that with the end sections they can produce system lengths of a maximum 4,500 m. The end sections can be designed in a whole variety of ways, for example monolithic or skeletal, cylindrical, conical, pyramidal etc. Crucial properties for load-bearing are that the base plate of the end piece should be practically distortion-free, with a high degree of solidity, finish quality and precision, and also systematic matching of all the individual parts and finishing processes.

The world's first use of structural tubular glass elements in building is the atrium facade of the "Tower Place" office building in London by Foster and Partners, which was completed in September 2002 (ill. 6). Here approx. 40 four metre long, centrally tempered system components with laminated glass tubes arranged in a 12 x 12 grid conduct the wind forces affecting the membrane-like curtain facade (the pressure and suction amount to + 50 kN per element) forces into the primary load-bearing system. For this reason, steel cables each prestressed at 75 kN are built into the glass components. The slenderness of these system components is about factor 24.
The best-known historical example of glass tubes in architecture are the "glass tube windows" in S.C. Johnson & Son Company's head office in Racine/ Wisconsin (1936 to 1939), by Frank Lloyd Wright. The structural components were designed ornamentally with glass tubes and are daylight-diffusing. But here the glass tubes did not have a statical function.
Other early examples of tubular glass elements in architecture have been forgotten, not least because safety aspects were not dealt with adequately. The latest development of laminated glass tubes is creating new possibilities for using glass as a building material: the advantages of skeleton construction can now be fully exploited in structural glass building. In this way, laminated glass tubes can expand the structural building element field and possibly contribute to realizing glass architecture fantasies that have remained fantasies until now.

6

7

8

Structural gluing –
A prototype glass shell

Werner Sobek
Lucio Blandini

The Institut für Leichtbau Entwerfen und Konstruieren (ILEK) at the University of Stuttgart has been researching the use of adhesive technology for joining glass for two years now, using double-curved glass shells. After a wide range of studies on glued glass panes, ILEK presented a spherical, glued glass shell to the public at "glasstec 202" (ills. 1,2). It is not just the use of gluing techniques that is new in this prototype, but also the use of chemical prestressing in the manufacture of curved glass panes. In the grid shells that have been used hitherto, for roofing historical courtyards, for example, the glass has been supported by a metal structure and is thus not part of the statical system. The grid shell thus impairs the visual effect made by the glazing, and the degree of transparency.

Glass as a primary load-bearing system
To achieve greater transparency, glass has to be used as the primary load-bearing component. Glass is an admirably pressure-loadable material and is specially suitable for double-curved shells that are exclusively pressure-loaded under their own weight because of their geometry.
"Glasbogen II", a research prototype dating from 1998 (ill. 3), proved that large loads could be dispersed with appropriate design criteria and a high residual stability guaranteed [1]. Extremely aesthetic and efficient roofs can be realized by using glass structurally. But until now only a few such structures have been built. In "Glasbogen II" the forces between the panes are transferred by metallic, point clamping systems to achieve maximum transparency. But this does raise two problems: the mechanical capacity of the glass is not put to its best

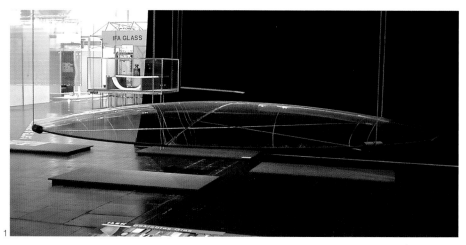

use because of the point connections, and the metal elements dominate the visual impression at the expense of transparency.

Gluing techniques

Gluing techniques offer an alternative here: the pane connection is no longer point, but linear, which makes maximum use of the rigidity of the glass.

A key feature when using gluing techniques is the aesthetic quality that can be achieved. As the joints are only a few millimetres thick and are noticeable only because of a small colour deviation, an area of glass can be designed without being visually impaired by frames and clamping strips.

Despite its great technical potential, this assembly technique has been little used so far: for example, silicon is used to glue the panes of a facade to the metal support structure (Structural Glazing), for example, to ensure a visually continuous glass envelope from the outside.

Gluing techniques have been used successfully for several years for structural jointing in mechanical engineering and vehicle construction. Much of the information about glue behaviour comes from the aerospace industry, where research has been conducted into alternatives to traditional jointing methods to meet the high safety and reliability demands. Today, structural elements in aircraft or vehicles are largely glued: it is thanks to gluing that vehicle windscreens now function as bodywork reinforcement elements. But only some of the knowledge and insights acquired are used in glass construction. In industry, the thickness of the adhesive used is a few tenths of a millimetre, and is not compatible with customary building tolerances. In most glass structures, adhesive 1 mm thick is adequates. But for butt gluing in glass shells the manufacturing and assembly tolerances rise to several millimetres. For this reason a series of experiments has been conducted to establish the effect of joint thickness on the mechanical behaviour of the adhesive.

The series of experiments

Extensive studies of glued impact joints for glass panes have been conducted in the central structural engineering lab at Stuttgart University. The available glues were tested for their ability to transfer the compression, thrust and, in part, tensile stresses in shells.

At first, twelve products were examined at 1 mm adhesive thickness. As there was little previous experience of gluing glass, it was urgently necessary to examine the glue/glass joint in detail. In a glued joint, a break can occur either at the point where the glass meets the glue (adhesion break, ill. 5) or within the adhesive itself (cohesion break, ill. 6). Adhesion breaks are the worst case, because the strength of the adhesive is not fully exploited. In contrast, in a cohesion break, the joint demonstrates maximum strength. The glass surfaces were roughened in the experiment to create a more efficient joint. Products that achieved high strength under tensile stress with 1 mm adhesive thickness were then examined with a 10 mm glued joint. The adhesives were acrylates, epoxy resins and polyurethanes. Silicons are already used in practice for structural gluing in structural glazing, but in butt joints they can transfer only small forces, and so they were not tested. Four products in all achieved a strong joint with greater adhesive thicknesses, and so they were then tested under shear loads. Here one acrylate is particularly significant, as in comparison with other adhesives it could take twice the tension, even though acrylates are suitable only for very thin joints.

The product showed minimal spreading in the five test bodies, and was only slightly sensitive to air bubbles and other irregularities. This quality is particularly important, as irregularities must not affect the strength of the joint when working with the adhesive. Hitherto, rigorous requirements when applying the adhesive have severely restricted the use of this jointing technique for building.

3

1   Glued glass shell prototype, "glasstec 2002", Düsseldorf Project group: L. Blandini, R. Brixner, B. Halaczek, J. Hennicke, K. Hummel, F. Lausberger, R. Wagner
2   Glued glass shell prototype, Workshop set-up
3   "Glasbogen II" prototype, "glasstec 1998", Düsseldorf

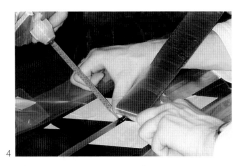

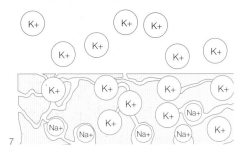

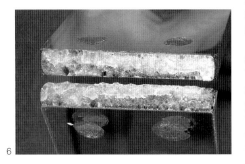

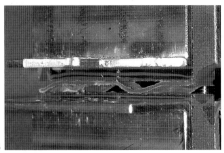

4 Gluing the prototype
5 Adhesion break in pull test
6 Cohesion break in pull test
7 Chemical prestressing principle
  Chemical state in glass (grey) after ion exchange

Suggested literature:

[1] Sobek, Werner; Kutterer, Mathias: Der Glasbogen
    auf der glasstec 1998. In: Kurzbericht 3/98.
    University of Stuttgart: Institut für Leichte Flächen-
    tragwerke. September 1998

The prototype

A prototype double-curved glass shell was developed for "glasstec 2002" in Düsseldorf to present the high mechanical and aesthetic quality of this kind of jointing to the public: the shell has a span of 2.35 m and consists of four spherically curved glass panes butt-jointed to each other.

The adhesive was able to meet the glass tolerances as expected and without any problems, so that the joint thickness varies between five and eight millimetres (ill. 5). The shell is suspended by cables from the ceiling at four points only (ill. 1). This both emphasizes the lightness of the hanging system and also the strength of the heavily loaded glued joints.

The curved glass panes were manufactured using a particularly innovative technology: one of the two panes of the laminated glass is only 2 mm thick and chemically prestressed.

Chemical prestressing

This technology meets significantly higher requirements than other manufacturing processes like float glass, for example, or thermally partially and fully tempered glass: significantly thinner panes can be used with the same load-bearing capacity and safety, thus reducing the material weight. For glass roofing, this makes extremely light and efficient constructions possible.

In chemical prestressing, the panes of glass are plunged into a bath of potassium salts to cause an exchange between the sodium ions in the glass surface and the larger potassium ions in the salt (ill. 7).

Unlike the usual thermal prestressing, this process can be carried out independently of the thickness and shape of the glass. As well as this, significantly higher stresses can be applied under normal conditions and when the glass is broken (residual stability). In the case of chemically prestressed glass the glass fragments when broken are sufficiently large to take certain forces (e.g. own weight). This is guaranteed by the overlap between the laminated glass pieces.

Looking ahead

The prototype glass shell used and presented several new technologies in the adhesive field that could revolutionize building with glass. After further tests for temperature stability, creep and ageing behaviour in the adhesives, it is possible to imagine these technologies being used successfully in all spheres where glass is used structurally.

Armoured laminated glass

Werner Sobek
Frank Maier

If laminated glass breaks, the structure remaining has a so-called "residual stability". This term is generally agreed to denote the resistance that a laminated glass component can still offer to prevent complete system failure – e.g. the collapse of the whole glass section.

It is vitally necessary to establish that the residual capacity is sufficiently high when using glass overhead, and in the case of glass for crawling or walking on. As many factors affect residual stability, it is very difficult to determine in advance. Factors influencing it include:

- the kind of glass used (float glass, partially tempered glass, safety glass)
- the laminated glass layering geometry
- the kind of intermediate layer (PVB, cast resin etc.)
- the kind of mount and load input
- the ambient temperature
- the fracture pattern in the damaged glass.

If these factors interact unfavourably there is a risk that the glazing will not have sufficient residual capacity. Residual capacity used to be determined by a simple homogeneous intermediate layer of polyvinylbutyral film (PVB).

In certain laminated glass structures (e.g. tempered safety glass/PVB/tempered safety glass), pure PVB membranes do not provide sufficient residual capacity in certain cases. This is particularly the case when the ambient temperature is high and the load is dispersed on one axis only. The reason for this is the properties of the PVB, which is a high-creep thermoplastic whose material properties are very temperature-dependent.

The Stuttgart University Institut für Leichtbau Entwerfen and Konstruieren (ILEK) has developed innovative reinforced/armoured laminated glass components to improve typical laminated glass residual capacity that can also sustain adequate loads in unfavourable conditions. The key development work on armoured laminated glass is described below.

1 Armoured laminated glass prototype, the PVB layer is armoured with a high-strength rust-resistant steel wire mesh.

2

2 Laminated glass with stainless steel mesh armour
3 Simplified residual stability endurance test with
two damaged laminated glass strips (in tempered
safety glass), front specimen: conventional with
non-armoured PVB, back specimen: armoured
laminated glass
4 Series of experiments on the possible use of armoured laminated glass components for steps
5 Semi-transparent metal armouring
6 Armoured laminated glass structure,
1 glass pane, 2 PVB membrane, 3 armour,
4 PVB membrane, 5 glass pane

*Load-bearing behaviour in damaged lami-
nated glass*
ILEK used numerous basis tests to inves-
tigate the mechanical properties of laminated glass, here particularly the load
dispersal mechanisms when fractured
[4].
One of the points established was that
laminated glass's residual stability is
based in principle on two key load dispersal mechanisms:

• Overlapping of glass fragments with
transfer of deflection through shearing
in the PVB membrane or support of the
fragments through adhesion forces vertical to the contact surface. This mech-
anism requires a certain minimum frag-
ment size of the kind that is usually produced by float glass or partially tempered glass.
• Transfer of tensile forces on the membrane plane. The fracture lines of the
two damaged glass layers are congru-
ently one above the other in this case,
or the glass layers are completely frac-
tionated, in other words made of tempered safety glass.

*Developing laminated glass with armoured
PVB layers*
In the latter load dispersal case
described, the bending strength and
load-bearing capacity of the damaged
glass components are very low. To raise
residual stability to an acceptable level it
is necessary to improve the strain resistance and tensile strength in the area of
the intermediate layer, which has hitherto
always consisted of a homogeneous PVB
membrane. This can be achieved by
embedding an armour-like reinforcement
in the PVB intermediate layer. Illustration
6 shows the construction principle for
armoured laminated glass of this kind,
with the armour laminated directly into the
PVB layer in manufacture.
The armoured elements that can be used
for this special application have to have a
very high tensile strength on the one
hand, but they have to be very thin, so
that a bubble-free and thus optically
impeccable intermediate layer is created.
Another particularly important aspect is
the transparency of the armour, as it is
usually important that it is still possible to
see through the glass. Illustration 6 shows
materials that meet these criteria well. It
shows meshes made of high-strength
spring and stainless steel wire and thin
perforated sheets.
Glass and carbon-fibre products can also
be embedded in the polyvinylbutyral layer

as armour and are suitable for this use.
Steel wire mesh is particularly interesting
for this use as it is available in a large
number of specifications.
Appropriate choice of wire thickness and
mesh size make it possible to adjust the
transparency of the mesh and the mesh
strength as appropriate.

*Armoured laminated glass with high resid-
ual stability*
A test programme was carried out on a
series of specimens, precisely quantifying
the residual stability of differently
armoured laminated glass [2, 3].
The test specimens were damaged in
advance as predefined, and then tested
for bending in a test machine. The specimens had to be damaged in advance in
such a way that the experimental results
can be reproduced and compared.
Hence the damage was done in terms of
the previously defined "transfer of tensile
forces in the membrane plane". The load-
bearing behaviour of the armoured layer
could thus be assessed directly. Load-
bearing capacity was tested identically in
specimens of non-armoured laminated
glass for comparative purposes.
The result was that the armoured specimens showed considerably greater bending strength as well as distinctly higher
residual stability.
As well as this, the addition of armour is
extremely effective. Very little material is
needed to achieve significantly greater
residual stability. Armour also clearly
improves load-bearing under continuous
stress. Building inspectors require a sur-
vival time of at least 24 hours when dem-
onstrating the residual stability of overhead glazing.
Illustration 3 shows a simplified endurance experiment with two damaged laminated glass strips. Both laminated glass
elements are made of tempered safety
glass. The specimen in the foreground is
made conventionally with non-armoured
PVB. It slid off the support under its own
weight a short time after the breakage of
the two tempered safety glass layers.
However, distortion is greatly reduced in
the armoured specimen that is still on top,
to the extent that it is possible to disperse
certain loads for several days and weeks.
Another positive quality that should be
mentioned is that after the load is
removed the specimen recovers its shape
to some extent.

3

4

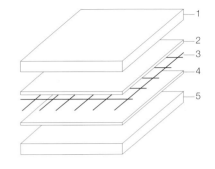

Practical applications
One particularly suitable field for using armoured laminated glass structurally is in glass constructions that have to meet particularly high residual stability requirements. This includes glazing that has to be walked on or at least crawled on to a limited extent for cleaning and maintenance purposes, and all overhead glazing.

A further series of tests was conducted on laminated glass building components in their original format to assess their suitability for common purposes like steps, for example [1] (ill. 4).

The individual step elements were line-supported on two sides and not clamped to the support, which means that the load can be dispersed by component bending alone. The distance between the supports was exactly 1 metre. The laminated glass elements were manufactured exclusively from tempered safety glass, the top and bottom layers of glass were each 4 mm thick, and the middle layer of glass was 12 mm thick. This meant that the steps were almost completely exploited statically. In the armoured specimen the armour was in the lowest intermediate layer.

A steel wire mesh was used in this particular case. After activating the impacting body several times and manual blows to the edges, all the individual panes in the laminated glass panels were damaged. The non-armoured reference element slipped and fell off the support immediately after sustaining the damage. But the armoured pane was able to sustain the load of 1 kN representing a person, and was observed in this state for 24 hours.

Optical effect of the armoured elements
Metal meshes produce different optical effects according to the mesh specification used. If a suitable wire thickness and mesh width are chosen, the mesh structure can no longer be made out by the naked eye. The amount of light passing through the pane can be controlled by the thickness of the mesh, i.e. the PVB armour can also provide sunscreening. This is particularly interesting in the case of overhead glazing (ill. 2).

The armour inserts can also be used as a design element. Carbon-fibre armoured laminated glass panes could be used as semi-transparent components in a glass screen, for example.

Suggested literature:

[1] OGI (FMPA), Baden-Württemberg: Untersuchung der Resttragfähigkeit von Verbundglaselementen mit Bewehrungsschichten, Forschungsbericht no. 25-27686. May 1999.
[2] Sobek, Werner; Maier, Frank; Kutterer, Mathias: Bewehrtes Verbundsicherheitsglas, Forschungsbericht 1/99. Universität Stuttgart: Institut für Leichte Flächentragwerke. June 1999.
[3] Sobek, Werner; Maier, Frank; Kutterer, Mathias: Tragverhalten von bewehrtem Verbundsicherheitsglas, Forschungsbericht 2/99. Universität Stuttgart: Institut für Leichte Flächentragwerke. October 1999.
[4] Sobek, Werner; Maier, Frank; Kutterer, Mathias: Versuche an Verbundsicherheitsgläsern zur Beurteilung der Resttragfähigkeit und des Verbundverhaltens. Forschungsbericht 1/98. Universität Stuttgart: Institut für Leichte Flächentragwerke. November 1998.

GRP-glass composite systems

Jan Knippers
Stefan Peters

Composite materials made up of glass-fibre-reinforced plastics (GRP) and glass is a central research topic at the Stuttgart University Institut für Tragkonstruktionen und Konstruktives Entwerfen, as this composite has a potential use of innovative facade structures. This is essentially because fibre-reinforced plastics offer high mechanical strength and low thermal conductivity. Also, the thermal expansion coefficient of GRP is very similar to that of glass. It is possible to make a direct composite of these two materials without great thermal stress. The own weight of the highly corrosion-resistant GRP elements is only quarter of the own weight of steel elements.

Fibre-reinforced plastics – material
Fibre-reinforced plastics are made up of two components: the fibres, which define the mechanical properties and the matrix surrounding them, which protects the fibres and fixes their position. Thermosetting plastics are usually used for the matrix. Thermoplastics are scarcely used in building at present. Both the reasonably priced and easily worked polyester resins and the more expensive epoxy resins are in widespread use as matrix materials. If chemical resistance is a key issue, then vinyl ester resins are used. If components need to have high thermal stability and low smoke generation in case of fire, phenol resins are recommended. Three materials have practical significance for reinforcement: glass, carbon and aramide fibres. Carbon fibres are used when very great strength is needed along with low weight. In terms of mechanical properties, a distinction is made between standard module fibres (HT), intermediate module fibres (IM) and high module fibres (HM).
Table 5 shows that carbon fibres are stronger and above all less prone to deformation than glass fibres. As they are so expensive, carbon fibres are very rarely used in building.
Aramide fibres have a part to play when very high impact resistance is needed, e.g. in bullet-proof vests.
The Institute restricted its research to glass as a reinforcing material for two reasons: carbon fibre is about ten times as expensive as glass fibre, and the thermal expansion ratings are very similar for glass fibre and glass, which makes a direct, rigid composite possible, while carbon and aramide fibres have negative thermal expansion coefficients.
In all fibre materials, the very thin, long elementary fibres are further processed

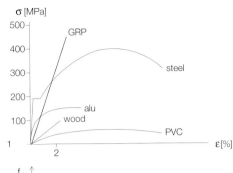

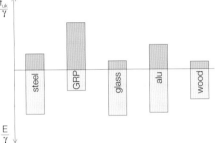

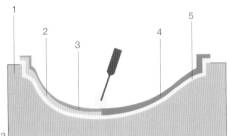

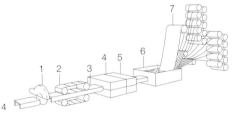

1 Stress-strain diagram with various materials
2 Qualitative comparison of tensile strength and rigidity in comparison with the own weight of various materials.
3 The laying-up principle
  1 mould, 2 woven fibre, 3 resin
  4 impregnated fibre, 5 release agent
4 Pultrusion principle
  1 saw, 2 caterpillar track, 3 profile
  4 heated mould, 5 pre-mould, 6 impregnation tank
  7 glass mat, 8 roving reels
5 Properties of various fibre types
6 Comparative material properties
7 Roof pane prototype with load
8 GRP composite support in bending test
9 FE mathematical models
  top: FE mathematical model for an test support
  bottom: FE mathematical model for a roof pane

to make rovings or threads. Rovings are skeins of 1,000 to 10,000 continuous fibres, placed together parallel, without twisting, to form one skein of thread. Glass, carbon and aramide fibres can be combined at will. Matrix and fibres can be further processed in various ways, with manufacturing techniques extending from manual work to automated manufacturing processes. One special feature of fibre-reinforced plastics is that the material actually comes into being only when the work acquires its form. Thus design has a considerable influence on material properties like strength or rigidity.

Manufacturing fibre-reinforced plastics
The simplest and oldest manufacturing process is laying up. The matrix and fibres are applied to a moulded shape by hand; fibre contents of up to 45 weight-% are possible. This is a low-investment manufacturing process used for making small quantities of freely shaped components (ill. 3). The quality of the material can be further enhanced by hardening the component under excess pressure, for example, in respect of higher fibre content and better surfaces. Another possibility for increasing fibre content for moulded parts in larger quantities is compression moulding with a two-piece heated tool. The use of sheet moulding compounds, resin-impregnated mats and meshes can improve the similarity of the products even further. For the building industry, manufacturing methods are needed that guarantee reproducible mechanical properties with high fibre content at low cost. Two methods are available for doing this at present: the wrapping technique, which is

used for making tubes and pipe elbows for the chemical industry, and the pultrusion method. In the latter, the fibres are drawn from the roller in one move through a impregnation bath with resin and then through a mould, and finally cut to length. This is a good way of making elements with a large variety of cross-sections. The glass fibre ratio is 70 weight-% (ill. 4). Elements of this kind are used for fixed members on off-shore platforms, for example, because of their high corrosion resistance and low maintenance requirements. The relevant material data for pultruded GRP profiles are presented comparatively in ills. 1 and 6. III. 2 shows that the advantage of GRP lies above all in the ration of tensile strength to own weight. But its low rigidity makes it unsuitable for constructions that need to be very slender.

7

8

9

5: Various fibre qualities

Fibre	tensile strength [MPA]	E module [Gpa]	Thermal expansion [10^{-6} K^{-1}]
E glass	2400	73	5
Carbon HT	3500	235	-0,5
Carbon HM	3600	474	-0,5
Aramide SM	2800	59	-2,3
Aramide HM	2800	127	-4,1

6: Comparative material qualities

Values	unit	GRP pultruded	steel S 235 JR	wood S 10	glass soda-lime glass	aluminium
Tensile strength	N/mm²	240	360	14	30–90	150–230
E-module	N/mm²	23000	210000	11000	70000	72000
Fracture strain	%	1–3	26			2–8
Density	g/cm³	1,8	7,85	0,6	2,5	2,7
Heat expansion coefficient (longitudinally)	10^{-6}/K	9	12	~4,5	8–9	23

10

10   The roof panes are placed on the wall panes
      on a 6 x 20 mm Dow Corning DC 993 silicon joint.
11   Glass pavilion, "glasstec 2002", Düsseldorf
      Design, statics, construction, assembly:
      University of Stuttgart ITKE, Prof. Jan Knippers
      Project direction: Stefan Peters
      Workshop management: Michael Tondera
      Project group:
      Shhiber Shhiber, Jürgen Müller, Marc Remshardt,
      Wolfgang Schnürich, Volker Scholz
      Glass: Interpane Glasgesellschaft, Lauenförde/P.
      GRP elements: Fiberline Composites; Kolding,
      Denmark
      Silicon adhesive: Dow Corning, Wiesbaden
      Assembly: Mirotec Glas- und Metallbau,
      Wettringen
      Test structure: Glasbau Galetzki, Stuttgart
      Consultants: Lehmann und Keller Ingenieure,
      Lauffen

GRP-glass composite systems

The specific properties of both materials are demonstrated in composite GRP and glass structures in buildings' external envelopes.

The high tensile strength of GRP elements makes them ideal as reinforcement for glass structures under tensile stress. Their poor conductivity also makes structures possible in which the load-bearing structure penetrates the thermal envelope or is on the same plane. In addition, the similar heat expansion figures for pultruded GRP elements and glass mean that they can be statically bonded with adhesives. Further advantages are the light weight of the GRP elements, their corrosion resistance and the comparative ease with which they can be worked.

The feasibility of a GRP-glass composite support was investigated in a series of experiments. First, various adhesives were tested for suitability in simple shearing tests.

The silicon adhesive DC 993, which was used for the pavilion, showed forgiving cohesive shear-off in the adhesive joint, with reproducible strengths. Additionally, silicon adhesives can be dissolved, which is an advantage for temporary structures. And years of experience about use in building are also available. However, silicon is very soft and does not achieve very high strengths (DC 993 permissible stresses: tension max. 0.14 MPA, shear max. 0.11 MPA). So silicon is not ideal for statical bonding between a GRP elements and glass. A number of tension and shearing test are currently in preparation to establish the breaking strengths and rigidity of other adhesives. The composite support principle, with a sheet of glass on top in the compression area and a GRP element in the tension area, was examined in a 3 m long test beam. The results of a FE (Finite Elements) mathematical model were compared with the experimental results (ills. 8,9, top). The GRP T-beam (h = 105 mm) was glued to a float pane t = 8 mm, b = 500 mm. The silicon joint was 6 mm thick. With a span of approx. 2.7 m the fracture load was 1.1 t with a deformation of approx. 100 mm third points.

Prototypes

The pavilion at "glasstec 2002" in Düsseldorf demonstrated statical reinforcement of glass by gluing GRP elements on to them (ill. 11). It consists of 6 panes at 6 x 2.5 m and six pultruded GRP members in fibre-reinforced plastic ending 25 cm before the support. The haunched T-beams were cut to size from a double-T element and stuck to the panes from below. The wall panes are 2 x 10 m float laminated glass. Partially tempered laminated glass was needed for the roof panes because of the large bending stresses near the ends of the members. Each pane weighs 750 kg (ill. 10). One roof pane was set up as an experiment before the pavilion was assembled (ills. 7,9, bottom). The gluing was undertaken under building site conditions. The results of the preliminary experiments also served to establish sound statical calculations. The ITKE is currently planning to develop a large-scale GRP-glass facade element. The structural potential and the building-physical efficiency of this new building method will be further investigated, with architecture students and building physicists, and by building further prototypes.

11

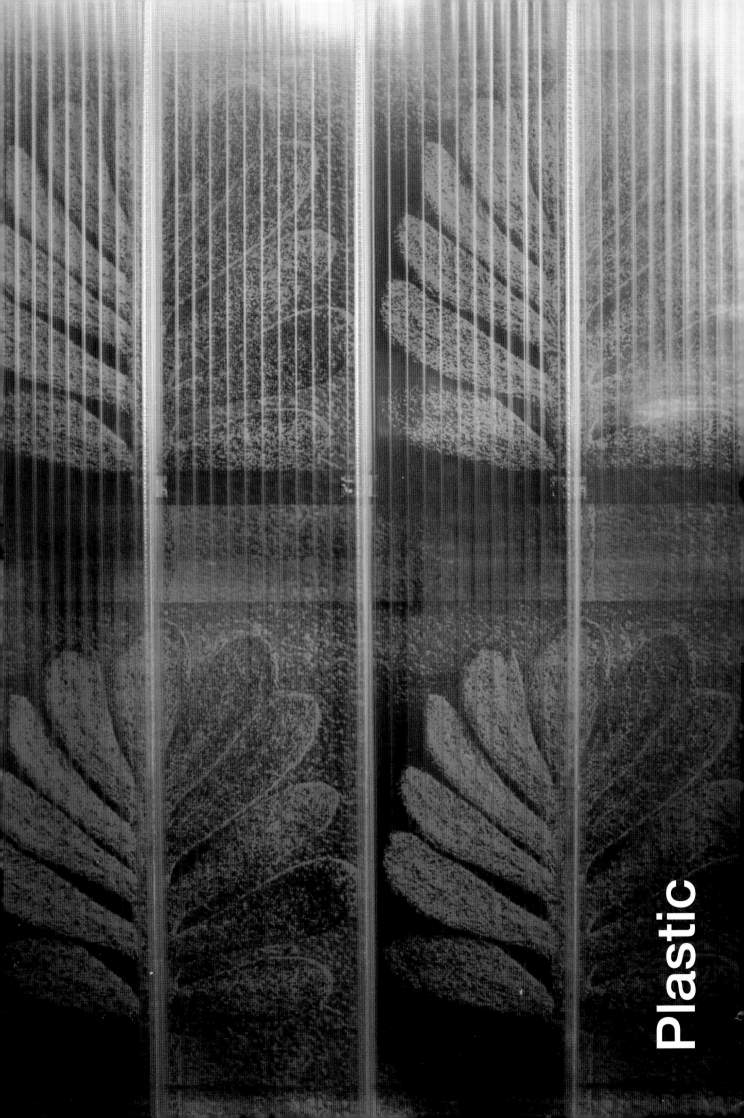

Plastic

Plastic – Translucent semi-finished sheet products

Frank Kaltenbach

Plastic products are well established in architecture. They often offer advantages over mineral glass when qualities like light weight, high loadability and low cost are needed. Until a few years ago there was a partially justified prejudice that many plastics discolour and so should be seen as low-value, short-lived products. Now, however, the new UV stabilized materials are seen as the essence of contemporary architecture. They are not just sought after for temporary exhibition structures, but also for long-term solutions. Warehouse facade become large-scale, printed works of art, corrugated sheets adorn museums and make lighting effects possible day and night. In 1992, Rem Koolhaas clad the roof of the "Kunsthaal" in Rotterdam with sheets of corrugated fibre-glass. The most recent example of plastic interpreted architecturally, colour and light on a large scale, is the envelope of the Laban Dance Centre in London, by architects Herzog & de Meuron.

To a considerable extent, the improved image of plastics is due to constantly improving quality and the wide range of materials available, which makes a broader range of uses possible. Because they can be handled in so many ways, when semi-finished products like solid sheets or bridging elements are processed, many of the undesirable qualities inherent in the material - within reason, of course - can be minimized and positive qualities emphasized. So the characteristics of the many different source materials on the market start to overlap. Brittle materials are toughened, and medium combustibles can be made fire-retardant. The term "transparency" is usually associated with a "crystal clear" view through mineral glass. But there are amorphous plastics – so-called "organic glass" – that to some extent more transparent that silica glass. The major diaphanous plastics used in the building industry that are on the market as semi-finished sheet products are introduced below.

What are plastics?
The term "plastics" covers organic materials with chain-like macro-molecular structures made either by transforming natural products (semi-synthetic plastics) or by synthesizing primary petroleum, natural gas or coal products (table 3). They consist of organic chemical elements: carbon (C) and hydrogen (H); oxygen (O), nitrogen (N) and sulphur (S) can also be involved. The term "organic" also implies similar qualities to those of materials that grow organically like wood, horn and resin.

Victor Regnault successfully made polyvinyl chloride (PVC) in the laboratory in 1838, by exposing vinyl chloride to sunlight. The German term "Kunststoff" (lit.: "artificial material"; "plastic") dates from the emergence of the magazine of the same name in 1911.

How is transparency explained?
Intermolecular forces – in plastics these are usually only Van de Waals forces – partly explain the material's physical qualities. These forces mean that there is a temperature for plastics at which they pass from a solid via a pasty to a liquid state. There are no precisely defined melting and boiling points.

- If the macro-molecules are convoluted like a felt, the condition is knows as amorphous. Amorphous plastics are glass-like, transparent and usually brittle.

- If the chain molecules are completely parallel over certain lengths, these areas are called crystallites. The rest of the length of the molecular threads consists of pliable loops, while crystallites are opaque.

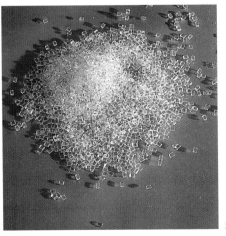

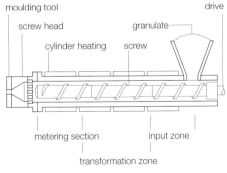

moulding tool · drive
screw head · granulate
cylinder heating · screw
metering section · input zone
transformation zone

1 Polycarbonate granulate
2 Schematic diagram of an extrusion machine
3 The plastics range (selection)

• Partially crystalline plastics like polyamides, PET and PTFE are more thermally stable than amorphous ones. When pigmented with soot or coloured pigments as UV protection they are opaque.

Thermoplastics, elastomers, thermosets
These plastics are technically defined and categorized under DIN 7724:

• Thermoplastics have unlinked, linear or branched macromolecular chains. They can be melted, welded and shaped three-dimensionally when heated. The thermoplastics group contains the most simply composed plastics like polyolefine PE and PP, and also PVC, PS and PMMA.

• Elastomers on the other hand are coarse-meshed three-dimensionally, rubber-elastic and cannot be shaped.

• Thermosets have a rigid three-dimensional structure. They change this structure only imperceptibly when heated, and maintain their rigid state until thermal decomposition Like elastomers, thermosets cannot be melted and thus cannot be welded. As unsaturated polyester systems they are usually reinforced with glass-, carbon- or natural fibres (GRP, CFRP).

Manufacture
Most synthetic plastics are derived from crude oil, representing 8 % of all crude oil production. The crude oil is distilled in the fractionating column and breaks down – according to the different boiling points – into gas, raw gasoline, diesel, heating oils and gas oil. They are all hydrocarbons and differ in the size and shape of their molecules.

The most important fraction for plastic manufacture is raw gasoline (naphtha). It is thermally broken down in the so-called "cracking process" and converted into ethylene, propylene, butylene and other hydrocarbon compounds. This also produces other raw materials used in plastics manufacture like for example benzene. Styrene is derived from ethylene and benzene, and vinyl chloride from chlorine and ethylene. Both monomers are source materials for other plastics like PVC, for example.

From monomer to polymer
There are three plastic synthesis processes for deriving macromolecules from small-molecule substances: polymerization, polycondensation and polyaddition. Plastics are categorized as polymers, polycondensates and addition polymers according to these processes.

• Polymerization has been known since 1930. It is a chemical reaction at room temperature – usually using hardening and accelerating catalysts – that takes small basic molecules each with a double bond and builds a long molecular chain without by-products forming in the reaction. Ethylene is polymerized to polyethylene (PE), vinyl chloride to polyvinyl chloride (PVC), styrene to polystyrene (PS) and propylene to polypropylene (PP). But different unsaturated products like styrene acrylonitrite also polyermize with each other to form the co-polymer

SAN, a modified polystyrene. A "chain reaction" takes place in polymerization that is merely knocked on.

• Polyaddition was not achieved until 1937. It defines the attachment of multifunctional amines or of alcohols, carbon acids etc. to highly reactive molecular groups. Polyurethanes and epoxy resins are made by this process. Here too no reaction products split off.

• Polycondensation has been known since 1910. When manufacturing phenoplastistics (phenol resin PF), for example, low molecular reaction by-products like water and ammonia are separated. Here the hardening catalysts are acids or bases. The most important plastics made by this process are phenol-formaldehyde resins (phenoplasts), thermoset paints and casts resins made up of linked polyesters and the thermoplastic polyamides (nylon types) or linear polyesters.

From polymer to granulate
So that this moulding compound can be easily stored, transported, dosed and melted, the polymers are first made into granulates. Here the plastic moulding compound is pushed through a "multi-hole sieve" to form an appropriate number of strands. These are then quenched in a bath of water and processed into pellets a few millimetres long in the granulator.

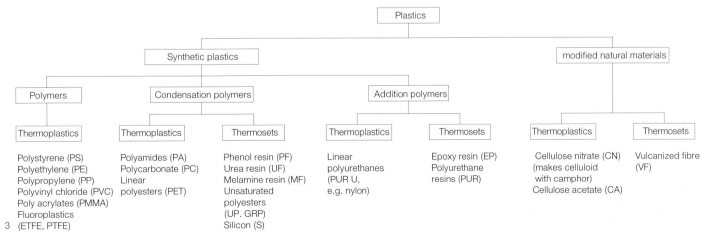

3

Extruding

The basic process for turning these pellets into semi-finished products is extrusion. Experiments began as early as 1935 to process a pulp of liquid softeners and PVC powder with large rubber-extruders. The extruder is like a mincing machine in which thermoplasts in granular form, more rarely in powder form, pass along a rotating screw through various temperature zones, where they are condensed, plasticized and homogenized (ill. 2).

Before the pellets go into the extruder they are dehumidified in the dryer for several hours at a temperature of 115 °C to avoid bubble formation when they are later heated. Precise granulate dosing is important; it is weighed out very accurately with the aid of conveyor scales or LBF systems. Ground material from shredded rejected products or recycling material can be mixed with the new batch. There are two possible colouring processes. Either the granulate has been coloured already by the manufacturer, or so-called "batch material", i.e. colour concentrates also in granulate form are mixed with the colourless moulding compound and the colorant when filling the extruder. In the first extrusion phase, the thermoplastics are melted by friction from the metal screw and additional heating of the cylinder. In the second phase, the viscous material is dehumidified under a vacuum at 250 °C and after the pressure increase zone filtered through a fine sieve (mesh diameter approx. 40 to 80 μm. At the end of the extruder, a gear pump is attached by an adapter. A second, small extruder can be added here, in which the base material is inseparably fused with very thin layers of other material in a so-called "co-extrusion process". This is used for UV protection layers, for example, or when infra-red reflecting layers are needed on PMMA or PC sheets. The adapter is attached to the nozzles that shape the semi-finished sheets. Thus single, double or multiple sheets emerge according to the shape of the nozzle. The completed sheets are coated with protective film and cut to shape. Theoretically, endless sheets would be possible, but building conditions, transport and fitting lead to standard sizes.

Calendering

Calendering is one of the commonest processes for manufacturing endless films in PVC for example. For solid elements, the melt emerging from the extruder nozzle is rolled (calendered) between mirror-polished rollers, with the distance between the rollers determining the thickness of the sheet. Different surface qualities make it possible to stamp patterns and make matt or structured sheets. The rolling temperature also determines the later degree of mouldability. Thus amorphous PVC is quenched with cold rollers, PC sheets are rolled hot.

Casting

The original glass-chamber casting process is available for PMMA manufacture, as well as extrusion. Historically speaking it is older than extrusion, but with current machines more modern technologically. With greater manufacturing effort it makes for higher performance products, particularly in terms of mouldability. The source material is not a polymer, as in the granulate, but the monomer MMA (methyl metacrylate) in watery, liquid form. First, viscosity is reduced to a more sluggish syrup (18 % of the material is already polymerized). In precise controlled quantities, this syrup is either coloured homogeneously with "batch granulate" in a stirring process, or passed in clear form into a chamber between two sheets of glass and distributed evenly. After the peripheral strip of the sandwich-like glass moulds has been closed, these are stacked one above the other in a polymerization chamber with air at 60 °C flowing round it, until 85 % of the material is polymerized. Complete polymerization is then achieved by quickly heating the air to 120 °C. Unlike extrusion, where only physical processes take place, a chemical reaction moving from monomer to polymer occurs in the glass chamber. The starter energy for polymerization can also be provided in the form of light, above all for thick, solid blocks. Using the most modern machines, large sheets up to a thickness of 25 mm can be manufactured as standard; these are used for sound insulation, for example. As a special product, for the transparent walls of deep-sea aquariums, for example, mono-blocks of 80 to 100 mm can be cast, to a maximum of 250 mm. The advantages of casting are that processing is simpler and the end products can be easily moulded, for example for sanitary use for bathtubs. Surface structures are achieved by exploiting the consistency of the glass used in the chamber, which determines the markings on the plastic. So etched glass in the chamber produces a matt sheet of PMMA.

Hollow shapes

Here the extrusion blowing process, the injection moulding blowing process or the centrifugal process can be used.

Injection moulding, foaming, pressing

Injection moulding is very widespread, because precision moulded parts, like for example car reflectors, can be manufactured, usually without any post-processing. Foaming, along with injection moulding and extrusion, is a process for making foam plastics. Foam materials manufactured from polymerizates (PE, PS, PVC), poly-condensates (phenolic, urea and expoxy polyester resins) and poly-adducts (PUR) are much used in the building industry for insulation. Polyester resins are polymerized to GRP sheets by hot pressing.

From semi-finished to end product

Semi-finished products manufactured by a primary process can be further modified. Sheet material can be drawn or blown for light domes. Additional surface treatment like printing, painting or metal vapour-coating are also possible. Florian Nagler's laboratory building in Bobingen (ill. 4) shows that prestigious architecture can be created without any additional tricks.

Materials and properties

The key transparent plastic sheets and their properties are listed below:

PMMA	Polymethyl methacrylate
PC	Polycarbonate
GRP	Glass-fibre reinforced plastic
PET	or PETA, amorphous polyethylene therephthalate
PETG	Glycol modified polyethylene terephthalate
PVC	Polyvinyl chloride
PS	Polystyrene
SAN	Styrene acrylonitrite
HPL	High Pressure Laminates

4

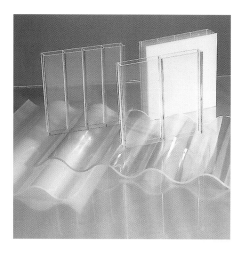
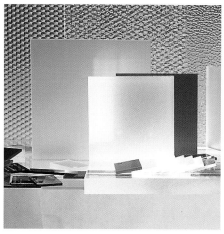
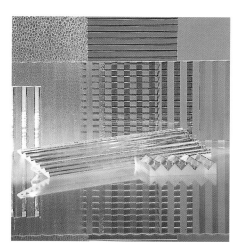

PMMA – polymethyl methacrylate

PMMA or acrylic glass has the best optical properties of all the polymers, and that at half the weight of glass. Light transmission in 92 % in a sheet 3 mm thick (according to DIN 5036, part 3). Because it allows light to pass throughout the spectrum it is ideally suited for greenhouses and the daylight technology field. Light transmission can be varied according to colour from 0 % at black via yellow approx. 24 % to 92 %. PMMA is permanently weather- and UV-resistant. Hence dyed elements hold their colour even outdoors.

Cast sheets can be can be more vigorously moulded than extruded material, which is important above all in the sanitary field, for bathtubs, for example. It exists in standard form up to 25 mm thick for uses like noise barriers on bridges (UV-impermeable, partly flame retardant and with integrated PA threads), where low own weights, high transparency and low fragility are needed. Cast monoblock material is used among other things for deep-sea aquariums (with a thickness of 80 to max. 250 mm). As a rule PMMA is normally flammable (DIN 4102 - B2). For uses like the roof of the Olympic Swimming Pool in Munich (see p. 99), less flammable cast sheets (DIN 4102 - B1) are available. To make this, acrylic glass sheets 11.5 cm thick are heated homogeneously to 150 °C, enlarged by 70 % in length and width by stretching and reduced to 4 mm thick. As a result of this manufacturing method the sheets shrink to their original size when heated and pull back from the seat of the fire (memory

effect), thus reducing the fire load. PMMA cellular and corrugated sheets are highly transparent, can be co-extruded with UV and IR protective layers and coated against condensation water drips. They are normally flammable. Solid PMMA sheets can be bent cold if certain minimum radii are considered, for tunnel vaults, for example. Their heat deflection temperature is higher than copolymers like PET. The maximum temperature for use is +70 °C for extruded and +80 °C for cast material, and thus lower than that of PC, but it is perfectly adequate for most architectural purposes. PMMA is hard, easy to work (comparable with hardwood) in a dry condition (the weight increase after water storage is a maximum 2 %), but if handled improperly it is prone to stress cracks. Drills and milling heads should be specially polished, and circular saw blades coated with hard metal; quite unlike PET-G, which can simply be nailed. The scratch-proof, high-gloss surface can be repeatedly renewed by polishing with special pastes. Length change through heat is approx. 8.5 times greater than glass, for which reason clamping should be preferred to drilling and screwing. Other use areas are solarium tops, where colour fastness is needed, as a clear, coloured or fluorescent light source for peripherally lit, energy-saving, extremely flat illuminated signs, anti-reflecting surfaces for picture-glazing or mirror surfaces.

Decorative versions for furniture construction, with a greenish edge image or "sand-blasted" optics are scarcely distin-

guishable from glass. Sound baffles as subsequent measures in concert halls are often made of PMMA. 80 % of the strength of the basic material can be achieved when gluing with polymerization adhesives. The uses here are for windows and model-making, where joints have to be invisible. In daylight technology, PMMA appears in the form of vertical light prisms or louvres that can be aligned horizontally. The key feature here is to adjust to the particular elevation of the sun (always 90° to the incident direction), to prevent rainbow effects from refraction. The prisms are made using an injection moulding technique, so that the surface is more precise than for extrusion. Using another principle, daylight is deflected and dispersed on linear horizontal air slits inside the PMMA sheet. PMMA is also used for translucent heat insulation (see page 24), in the form of clear or white capillary tubes.

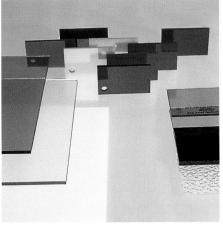

PC – polycarbonate

PC's uses include protective cladding and cold-bend tunnel vaults, because of its high thermal stability and indestructability as a result of mechanical influence. In the short term, maximum use temperatures lie at 150 °C without load, and in the long term at 80 to 120 °C. PC is 250 times more impact resistant than float glass of the same thickness. The izod core impact test at 23 °C is 30 to 40 times higher than that of a normal PMMA sheet. PC is hail-proof from a thickness of 1 mm. There are versions with particularly scratchproof coatings whose material-inherent mechanical robustness is higher still, also with fibre-glass reinforcement for additional rigidity as a construction material. The basic material is fundamentally UV stabilized and therefore not approved for use with foodstuffs, with certain exceptions. PC is permanently weather-resistance, but discolours if untreated. For outdoor use it is co-extruded with a UV protection layer on one or both sides.

PC is available, dependent on the moulding material, without flame protection in fire classes B1 and B2 (DIN 4102) and self-extinguishing on removal of the ignition source.

Light transmission is a maximum 88 % for clear sheets 3 mm thick, and approx. 35 to 50 % for white sheets. PC has glass-clear transparency with a high surface gloss and can carry great depth of colour in transparent, translucent and dense states. Hollow cellular sheeting, corrugated sheets, corrugated cavity elements, panels and light-transmitting pantiles are among the semi-finished prod-

ucts available. As an impact-resistant upper shell, PC can be combined with PMMA shells underneath it for multi-shell light-domes. Its uses include vandal- and bullet-proof police shields, stadium roofs or showcases. For translucent heat insulation, PC capillary tubes and special hollow cellular sheeting are preferred where the ambient temperatures are too high for PMMA. e.g. under non-back-ventilated translucent dressing. PC hollow cellular sheeting are available in lengths to over 18 m and are secured with the usual post-and-rail trim moulding.

There are tongue-and-groove systems on the market for externally flush facades without visible bracing, as in the 11.4 m high hollow cellular sheeting for the factory hall in Bobingen (ill. 4).

The thermal expansion coefficient of 0.065 mm/m K is eight times higher than glass. With an annual temperature difference of 50 K from winter to summer, this means 3 mm longitudinal expansion on the short side and 6 mm on the long side for a 1 × 2 m sheet. The bracing must be able to compensate for these movements. All the usual wood- and metal-working tools can be used for processing. Thin sheets are best cut with a knife.

GRP in UP – unsaturated polyester resins

Fibre-glass is used as a facade material when there is greater risk of breaking and absolute clarity of vision is not needed. The semi-finished materials are not extruded, but laminated: several layers of glass-fibre mats are bedded in resin, compressed and hardened under heat. Here the proportion of glass determines the tensile strength.

Natural discolouring as an effect of UV is avoided with coloured pigments or colourless acrylic components. To prevent the fibres becoming exposed by weathering, the surface has to be finished with additional fleece, reinforcement resin or paint.

Flat, corrugated and multi-layered hollow cellular sheeting (partially filled with insulating material) is secure against a thrown ball to DIN 18032 part 3, and can be worked with standard tools for metal.

There are naturally transparent or white-translucent versions with or without spun glass inserts. GRP conforms to fire protection group B2 (DIN 4102), or as a special form of the higher class V.2 in Switzerland. GRP is available in the form of corrosion-resistant highly loadable grids and also as decorative sheets with inlaid grasses.

Polyster resins are thermosets, hence re-use of the raw materials and remoulding under heat treatment are not possible. Burning with heat recovery is often the most environment-friendly means of disposal.

$$... - [O - \bigcirc - \underset{CH_3}{\overset{CH_3}{C}} - \bigcirc - O - CO -] ...$$

$$... - O - CO - \underset{\underset{CH - C_6H_5}{CH_2}}{\overset{\overset{CH - C_6H_5}{CH_2}}{CH}} - C - CO - O - CH_2 - CH_2 - ...$$

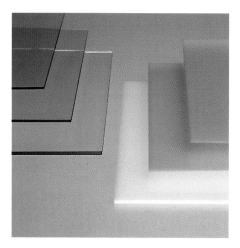
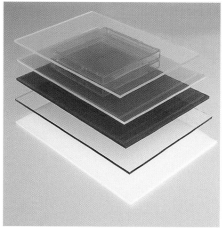
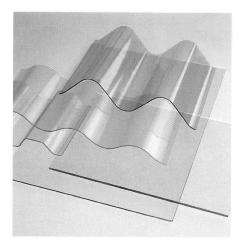

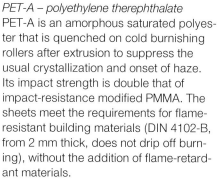

PET-A – polyethylene therephthalate
PET-A is an amorphous saturated polyester that is quenched on cold burnishing rollers after extrusion to suppress the usual crystallization and onset of haze. Its impact strength is double that of impact-resistance modified PMMA. The sheets meet the requirements for flame-resistant building materials (DIN 4102-B, from 2 mm thick, does not drip off burning), without the addition of flame-retardant materials.

Little smoke is developed in combustion, and no toxic gases are produced. However, the maximum temperature for use is only 65 °C. Because it is highly resistant to chemicals (better than PC), graffiti in shelters, for example, can be removed with acetone- and benzene-free solvent cleaners without impairing its optical or mechanical properties. PET-A is food compatible and easy to recycle.

The solid plastic sheets are clear, coloured, transparent or with a smooth or structured surface (coloured white or densely in crystalline form). They are outstandingly suitable for weatherproof curved glazing or tunnel vaults because of their excellent elasticity.

Swaging is possible at lower temperatures (120 °C) than for PC (180 °C), which reduces cost and energy consumption. Light transmission is 89 % in a sheet 4 mm thick, and processing and printing present no problems.

PET-A – polyethylene therephthalate
For this glycol-modified PET crystallization, in other words the parallel arrangement of the molecules, is prevented by introducing an inhibiting diol. Hence the material, which is partially crystalline as such, remains amorphous and thus highly transparent even at high swaging temperatures.

The impact resistance of this co-polymer is somewhat higher than that of PET-A and PVC, the service temperature area under mechanical stress extends from approx. -40 °C to 65 °C (PET-A: 20 °C to 65 °C). The heat deflection temperature of up to approx. 65 °C is greater than that of PET-A. It responds well to nailing, stamping, cutting with guillotine shears or with lasers, simple gluing and welding, and its outstanding swaging properties, make it ideal for home-workers and series production. PET-G is physiologically harmless without UV stabilization and is used in the food industry for food containers, and also in orthopaedic technology. Its even illumination and good printability make PET-G suitable for vandal-proof advertisement panels, display construction and for covering machines. PET-G is weatherproof in the long term with UV stabilization and optically stable. The material is difficult to burn (DIN 4102-B1). Pre-drying is not required as a rule, and hot deformation can be carried out at relatively low temperatures, which saves energy costs.

PVC – polyvinyl chloride
PVC sheets are used as a reasonably priced material in the form of corrugated or trapezoid sheets where no heat insulation is needed, for example for carports and stand roofs. The geometry of the corrugations matches commercial coverings in other materials like fibre cement sheets and make flush connections possible. PVC has a thermal expansion coefficient 11 times higher than glass, hence sufficient play has to be built in when fixing. The service temperature runs from 0 °C to 60 °C, and it is necessary to guarantee that the material cannot overheat, by providing sufficient back-ventilation, for example.

UV stabilization is possible today without lead, barium or cadmium additives. The UV layer is available clear, bluish or bronzed. With material thicknesses of approx. 1 mm, light transmission is 85 %. Special products have enhanced impact resistance and higher bond strength for printing ink. Lit signs can also be manufactured with paint and laminated film. PVC sheets are suitable for outdoor use only to a limited extent in terms of colour fastness, as colours can change over time.

PVC is recyclable and difficult to burn (DIN 4102-B1). The fire gas hydrogen chloride can produce hydrochloric acid among other products while fire is being extinguished, but resultant corrosion is very rare.

$$...[-CO-\bigcirc-CO-O-CH_2-CH_2-O-]...$$

$$HO-CH_2-\bigcirc-CH_2-OH$$

$$...[-CH_2-CH-]...$$
$$\quad\quad\quad Cl$$

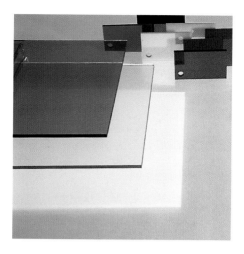

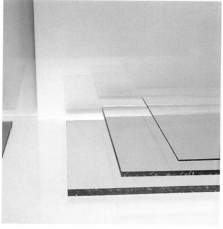

PS – polystyrene

PS and PVC, unlike the technical plastics (PMMA, PET, PA) are commodity plastics. PS is used mainly for translucent areas in interior spaces.

The benzene ring in the building block inhibits build-up of the macro-molecules. This produces both rigidity and transparency, but also results in brittleness.

The basic types include varieties that are treated with antistatic, stress crack resistant, or capable of injection moulding, extrusion and extrusion blowing through the addition of blowing agents. The maximum service temperature is 80 °C. But PS is readily flammable without flame retardants (DIN 4102-Bs), burns brightly with a very sooty flame).

The extrusion process can be used to produce a large number of colours and designs as well as the extruded, transparent, anti-reflectant and translucent white standard products. In the standard version the sheets are UV stable and retain their colour for years as long as they are used indoors for purposes like shower doors, non-reflecting picture frames, light panels or exhibition stands.

The advantages of PS are its reasonable price, low specific weight of 1.05 g/cm³ (PET-A: 1.34 g/cm³), high transparency (90 % at a thickness of 3 mm), good chemical stability and low water absorption, along with very good electrical qualities and recycling possibilities.

SAN – styrene acrylonitrite

If two of the five styrol building blocks in the homo-polymer polystyrene are replaced with acrylonitrite, this produces the co-polymer SAN. This molecular reconstruction leads to improved properties vis-à-vis PS, i.e. greater rigidity (special forms are also available with 35 % of the moulding compound in the form of fibre reinforcement), hardness, scratch resistance, toughness, thermal shock resistance (maximum service temperature: 90 °C) and resistance to oil, fat and aromatic substances, and also to stress cracking. But SAN is inferior to polystyrene in its electrical properties, and it absorbs more water. The yellow cast of the source material is enhanced by the addition of blue dye, which produces glass-clear transparency (light transmission is 88 % at a thickness of 3 mm). Other dyes produce translucent and opaque versions. SAN is used outdoors for illuminated signs, industrial doors, greenhouses, caravan equipment etc. Versions without UV stabilizers can be used for flat or curved shower cubicles and are food-grade items. SAN is easy to process by vacuum moulding and soft bending. It will take print in the form of letterpress, letterflex, dry offset, lithography, heliogravure and screen printing. Abrasion wear can be minimized by applying thin coats of clear varnish.

HPL – High Pressure Laminates

These 1.6 mm thick, translucent High Pressure Laminates (HPL) are made up of coloured decorative papers impregnated with melamine resin. They are used as back-lit surfaces, and can be built into cupboards, for example, vertically or horizontally or slightly curved, in frames. The high proportion of melamine makes the panels brittle, and a great deal of care is needed when working with them.

The opaque version 1.2 mm thick is conceived as a composite panel. It is pressed with kraft paper impregnated with phenol resin, polished on the back and can be applied to a stress-free support material like plywood panels, for example. These panels are not translucent, but give a sense of three-dimensional depth. Before being put to use, the laminated panels and their support materials have to be preconditioned at the same time at a controlled temperature and humidity. The panels are only suitable for indoor use, and the surfaces are not very scratch resistant. The 1.6 mm thick material expands up to 3mm/m longitudinally and up to 6 mm/m laterally. To avoid stress cracks, felt or rubber washers should be used, and adequately large drill sizes allowed for.

Abrasive cleaners can impair the surface. The material should not be used in the immediate vicinity of heat sources. The direction of the fibre structure should be considered when processing and fitting the panels.

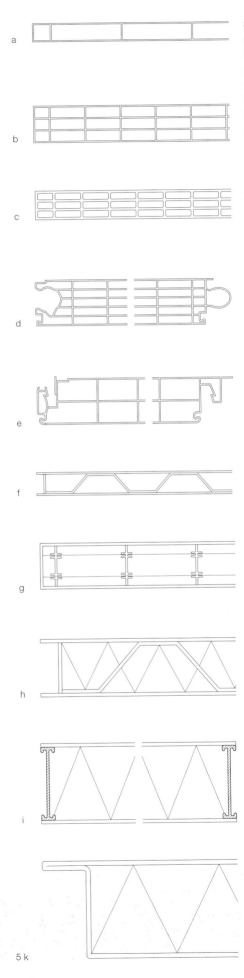

a

b

c

d

e

f

g

h

i

5 k

Standard requirements for semi-finished products

Because of the wide range of often competing requirements, the standard range of sheet plastics consists mainly of hollow cellular sheeting and corrugated or trapezoid sheets. The requirements are as follows:

Weight

The bulk density of PMMA (1.19 g/cm^3) and PC (1.2 g/cm^3) is approximately half that of glass. Thinner walls also mean support structures with smaller dimensions, and savings in transport and assembly. So extruded hollow cavity panels up to approx. 20 m long can be handled by only a few workers. GRP products are usually heavier than the other plastics (approx. 1.67 g/cm^3).

Statics

Diagonal supports make hollow cavity panels more rigid, though they do reduce the cold-bending radius. To reinforce the panels further, metal elements are pushed into the cavities or sheets of GRP are glued to aluminium frames to make panels. To reduce the support structure to a minimum, there are special elements with raised ribs on the market, or corrugations in the form of hollow cellular sheeting. The suction wind loading is considerably higher at the periphery of buildings, so the span has to be reduced or tongue and groove joints replaced with trim mouldings. In the case of GRP sheets, rigidity is dependent among other things on the proportion of glass by weight. Thin corrugated PVC sheets are flexible and highly loadable, as they were drawn down in the factory from 3 mm to 1.5 mm thick. For the highest pressure loadings, like those in the transparent walls of deep-sea aquariums, for example, cast PMMA blocks up to 250 mm thick are used, with invisible glued joints.

Heat insulation

As plastic hollow cellular sheeting cannot be made airtight, evacuating the air-gap or filling it with inert gases does not produce permanent results. Hence the number of chambers was raised to five, to minimize convection in the cavity. A sheet thickness of 40 mm treated in this way makes U-values around 1.2 W/m^2 K possible. Sheets can have selective active materials co-extruded on to their outside that reflect the infrared sunlight wavelength outwards in summer and the heat radiation inwards in winter. The GRP cavities in a product are made into hollow cellular sheeting with two films. Other firms fill the cavity with spun glass inlays, film layers made from renewable raw materials or aerogel granulate. The last achieves a U-value of 0.4 W/m^2 K for sheets 5 cm thick.

Sound insulation

Sound insulation is particularly important in industrial building when the aim is to minimize sound emissions to the outside of the building. For this reason, one manufacturer makes GRP panels with reinforced covering layers, and fills the gap between the sheets completely with a translucent spun inlay. The sound insulation achieved, R´w is up to 34 dB (A) for sheets 70 mm thick. Glazed sound insulation screen on motorway bridges are produced in 15–25 mm cast or extruded PMMA. Polyamide fibres are cast in to prevent fragments from falling out.

Weather protection

PMMA is the only material that does not need additional protection against the weather. Hence its use as a co-extrusion layer to protect the surfaces of other artificial glass on one or both sides. UV-protected PC, PVC, PET, PETG and GRP products can be used outdoors with long-term guarantee periods of 10 years, in Central Europe at least. The edges of some products have to be covered, however. Special films or gel coatings prevent GRP sheets from early discoloration and revealed fibres.

Technical light properties

PMMA is the material with the highest light transmission. Special light-dispersing, colour-faithful PMMA sheets have recently come on the market for LED advertising, permitting construction depths from 40 mm. Colour-neutral diffuser particles embedded in acrylic glass raise the luminous intensity of shallow light areas lit via the edges. A large distance between the cells, "No Drop" coating on the outsides and in the cavities create maximum through-vision and UV permeability in PMMA hollow cellular sheeting. A special UV-impermeable acrylic glass is available to avoid fading of glazed-in images; satinized surfaces are effective against unwanted reflection. The other transparent plastics are more or less UV-impermeable in their own right. Light transmission and glare can be effectively reduced with an IR-reflecting layer, structuring or tinting. PETG has high brilliance, compared with PMMA

5a–k: Hollow cellular sheeting elements in different materials and brands – For manufacturers see the second column in the table. The selection makes no claim to completeness. Products of comparable quality are available from other manufacturers in some cases. The recommended prices are non-binding and are to be seen as pure material costs excluding VAT and fitting.

PMMA	Polymethyle methacrylate	
PC	Polycarbonate	
PET	or PETA, amorphous polyethylene therephtalate	
PETG	Glycol modified polyethylene terephtalate	
PVC	Polyvinyl chloride	
GFK	Glass-fibre reinforced plastic	

	Material	Manufacturer	Product name	Illustration 5	Thickness in mm	max. width in mm	max. length in mm	heat transfer coefficient in W/m²K	Energy transmission efficiency g in %	Light transmission τ in %	Sound insulation factor R'w in db(A)	Fire protection class	Weight in kg/m²	Recommended price, approx. €/m²
flat sheeting	PMMA	Röhm	Plexiglas XT resist 100 — Impact resistance adjustable in stages to fracture-proof		4	2,050	3,050			91		B2	4.8	60
	PC	Makroform	Makrolon Mono dura clear — enhanced scratch resistance		4	2,050	3,050			89		B2	4.9	150
	PETG	Simona	Simollux-UV — fracture-proof, swaging without pre-drying		4	1,500	3,050			90		B1	5.1	35
	PET	Thyssen Schulte	Nudec PET-UV — grafitti-proof, more rigid than PETG, U protection		4	2,050	3,050			89		B1	5.32	50
	PVC	Simona	Simona PVC-Glas-SX transparent — enhanced impact resistance, unsuitable for outdoor use		4	1,000	2,000			66		B2	5.32	35
	GFK	Hahlbrock	Halusite 100 — spherically curved special shapes possible		5	2,000	3,500					B2	8.35	110
corrugated sheeting	PMMA	Röhm	Plexiglas resist farblos C struktur 76/18 — enhanced impact resistance, design structure		3	1,045	4,000			88		B2	4.0	30
	PC	Makroform	Makrolon onda multi longlife 2/177-51 — corrugated hollow cellular sheeting, rigid, UV protection		5	1,097	7,000	3.7	78	77		B2	2.0	17
	PVC	Solvay	Ondex, Sollux, 76/18 — light, reasonably priced, easy to manipulate		1.2	988	6,000			80		B1	2.0	15
	GFK	Scobalit	various corrugated and trapezoid shapes — compatible with opaque elements by other manufacturers		0.9	3,000	20,000			89		B2	20	20
hollow cellular sheeting	PMMA	Röhm	Plexiglas Alltop — clear, UV permeable, No-Drop	a	16	1,200	7,000	2.5	91	82	22	B2	5.0	45
	PMMA	Röhm	Plexiglas Heatstop S4P Weiß No-Drop — reflects IR radiation, No-Drop layer	b	32	1,230	7,000	1.6	30	40	24	B2	5.7	60
	PC	Makroform	Makrolon multi longlife 4/25-25 1140 IQ — reflects IR radiation, hail resistant, UV protection	c	25	980	11,000	1.6	24	30	22	B2	3.7	60
	PC	Rodeca	PC 2540-6, opal antiblend — tongue and groove jointing, available in two colours	d	40	500	11,000	1.15	45	45	22	B2,B1	4.2	100
	PVC	Rodeca	PVC 2340-3 — with co-extruded acrylic UV protective layer	e	40	300	11,000	1.65		67	21	B1	5.5	35
	GFK	Scobalit	lighting elements — diagonal cells for rigidity	f	20	2,400	8,000	2.6		78	20	B1,B2	5.3	95
	GFK	Butzbach	Varioplan plus, Farbton Brillant — clear material, crystal structure, 3 colours		40	486	15,000	2.6	42	78	25	B2	11.0	*
	GFK	Butzbach	Varioplan plus, Farbton Brillant mit 2 Zwischenfolien — * only available as individual facade system	g	40	486	15,000	1.6	42	63	27	B2	11.0	*
	GFK	Scobalit	Scobatherm Nanogel transluzent — aerogel filling, F 30	h	50	2,500	8,000	0.41	26	23	27	B1	12.0	340
	GFK	Brakel Aero	Grillodur zweischalig Naturton — GRP sheeting glued to aluminium element, can be walked on		70	2,000	5,600	1.56	69	77	25	B2	8.0	130
	GFK	Brakel Aero	Grillodur mit Glasgespinsteinlage — Enhanced sound and heat insulation, light dispersal	i	70	1,200	8,000	0.64	46	51	34	B2	10.0	150
	GFK	Scobalit	Scobatherm Moniflex — filling material: folded sheets of vegetable cellulose	k	85	935	3,000	0.62	48	39	28	B1	5.7	140

Plastic
Standardized half-finished products – requirements

a

b

c

d

seal

sealant

e

f

6

7

and PC, PVC hollow cellular sheeting seems slightly dull. Because of production conditions, GRP products are less transparent and give a diffuse light that does not produce sharp shadows, as required in the workplace in particular. Here the light transmission can be further reduced by the thickness of the sheet, the proportion of fibre and fillings.

Fire classification
In general, PVC, PET and PETG are in fire class B1, hardly flammable – and PC, PMMA and GRP to fire class B2 normally flammable (DIN 4102 part 1). But the approval does not apply to all thicknesses of material and semi-finished products, and must be sought in each case. Hence, individual products can be classified B1 by using special resins for GRP, introducing flame-retardants and dependent on the sheet thickness in the case of PC hollow cellular sheeting or the down-drawing of cast solid sheets in the case of PMMA. The sheets drip when burning differently or not burning, and are classed as "hard" or "soft" roofing (DIN 4102, part 7). Melt-out in case of fire (melt-out area according to DIN 18234) can be used to complement or reduce the need for smoke and heat extraction.

Mechanical stress
Traditionally, polycarbonate is the most impact-resistant plastic, followed by PETG. But modified PMMA can be used at various stages up to a very high impact strength. PVC sheets are less suitable under mechanical stress, but can be modified to make them more impact resistant to a limited extent. Special coatings raise the scratch resistance of solid PC sheets, and these are used for vandal-proofing. In the case of horizontal fitting, checks should be made whether breakage-resistant accessibility is required under ZH 1/44. Resistance to thrown balls under DIN 18032 part 3 and to pucks in sports halls should be matched to the sport to be played. Hail resistance cannot be taken for granted for all products, and can vary according to the size of the hailstones between partial and unlimited. For safety reasons, it can be necessary to make the translucent surfaces up to A3 high security standards (DIN 52290 V part 4). GRP sheeting meets most of these requirements.

Resistance to chemicals
Detergents, paint, adhesives and seals have to be compatible with the products.

Graffiti can be removed from PET sheets without trace, but this is not the case for all plastics.

Temperature range
PC products cover the greatest service temperature range, from -40 to 120 °C. PETG sheets are also highly impact resistant to -40 °C, but should not be permanently exposed to temperatures over 65 °C. PVC sheets soften above 60 °C, PMMA tends to crack in heat, hence there should be good back ventilation and light-coloured support structures.

Processing
Soft materials like PVC or PET are suitable for fine cutting-to-size. Hollow cellular sheeting in all materials is closed in the factory at the end or all round, which minimizes liquid absorption and damage during transport or fitting. Cutting to length and adaptation can not longer be carried out on the building site.

Mounting
It is important that all plastics are mounted free of secondary bending and with flexible seals. With a temperature difference of 50 K, material-dependent length changes occur from 3 mm to 5 mm per running metre, and this has to be accommodated with by appropriate play when drilling, and for clamping and edging elements. Corrugated sheets are mounted at the apex of the wave, and in the valley on walls. No spacers should be used for corrugated PMMA sheeting, to avoid binding noises.

Recycling
GRP products are burned in refuse incineration plants; the other materials can be returned to the production process as granulate. Used material should be handed in to manufacturers or recycling firms.

8

6 Current corrugated sheet profiles:
   a w/h = 76/18 mm
   b w/h = 94/35 mm
   c w/h = 130/30 mm
   d w/h = 177/51 mm special version as hollow cellular sheeting
   e fixing corrugated sheeting to the roof: fixing on the wave crest
   f to the wall: fixing in the wave trough
7 Institute in Grenoble
   Material: clear polycarbonate corrugated sheeting, installed vertically
   Architects: Lacaton Vassal, Bordeaux
8 Studio in Madrid
   Material: white corrugates sheeting installed horizontally
   Architects: Abalos und Herreros, Madrid

Individual design possibilities

Manufacturers of standard semi-finished sheeting also exploit the advantage of being able to modify plastics to meet particular requirements. Many of the features that are merely technically motivated, like iridescent, shimmering infra-red layers or corrugated hollow cellular sheeting are used for creative reasons alone. Often special requests lead to the creation of new products, which then go into series production. There are many ways of optimizing a semi-finished plastic product technically or making it creatively individual even at the manufacturing stage:

Thickness of material
Wall and panel thickness, or weight per unit area, are influenced by statics, mechanical strain, and sound insulation or fire protection factors.

Design
Translucent materials can be cold-bent, thermoformed or swaged. PETG absorbs little liquid under swaging, and therefore does not have to be pre-dried as a rule. On the other hand, roof or facade sheeting is usually cold-bent. The sheeting is delivered flat to the building site, fitted to the curve of the support structure and screwed into place. Typical uses are tunnel vaults for shelters and entrance canopies. Minimum bending radii have to be kept to, according to the material used. In the case of relatively rigid and weather-resistant PMMA sheeting the minimum bending radius (without modifier) is 330 times the thickness of the sheeting, for the more impact-resistant polycarbonate 150 times and for PET 120 times. But for PET (without modifiers) the sheeting thickness has to be considerably raised because of the lower service temperature and poor creep behaviour under load to achieve safety values comparable with PMMA or PC. For 15 mm thick polycarbonate sheeting this means a minimum radius if 2.25 m. If lower minimum radii are used, the sheeting has to be thermoformed.
Laminated sheets are shaped to meet demand in their "inner life" (ills. 5a-k). Different cavity cellular sheeting profiles influence rigidity, heat permeability and light transmittance. Some manufacturers produce tongue and groove butt joints, which make for homogeneous surfaces without fitting strips (ill. 18). Specially shaped corrugated sheeting makes it easier to connect to rising walls and roof beams, or enable better rainwater drain-age at verge flashing and eaves. Trapezoid and corrugated sheeting with identical geometry to commercial opaque metal or fibre-cement sheeting can be combined with these as occasional light areas. Light domes are available in round, rectangular and pyramid shapes.

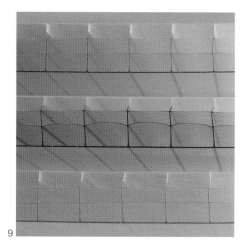

Co-extrusion
During the extrusion process, additional layers, e.g. UV protection or an infra-red reflecting layer are fused with the element. This can be on one side, e.g. the outside or on both sides. Purely creative effects are also available through co-extrusion (ill. 9). The outside of the polycarbonate hollow cellular sheeting at the Laban Dance Centre in London is made up of three crystal-clear layers. The layer on the room side was co-extruded in white, green, blue or red, to achieve a translucent, coloured shimmer from the outside (ill. 9). This air-permeable plastic is 60 cm away from the milk-glass insulation glazing. It is not possible to look into the facade cavity because of the translucent materials. The facade seems like a light-emitting body from both the outside and the inside (architects: Herzog & de Meuron, Basel).

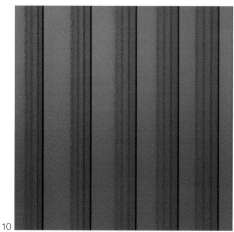

Structuring
Materials, like GRP elements in this case, that are originally transparent, can diffuse light through honeycomb, wrinkle or rib structures, for example (ill. 11). As a textured surface makes cleaning more difficult, the structure in often stamped on to the internal cells in the case of PC hollow cellular sheeting (ill. 10) or is mounted on the inside in the case of corrugated sheeting. Structures are used for sight protection, light dispersal or as design elements. Satinized acrylic glass surfaces reduced reflection in picture glazing.

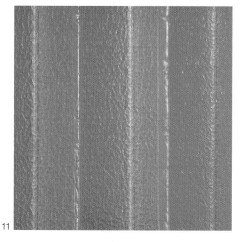

Casting
Technical modifiers, stabilizers and colour pigments can be cast into the material or added before the granulate is extruded. In the case of less intensely tinted hollow cellular sheeting, the ends of the cells cast a pin-stripe image on the outer wall (ill. 9). As well as the brown shades customary for PMMA and PC sheeting, it is also possible to obtain blue hollow cellular sheeting, as used among other places for the Estonian pavilion at Expo 2000 in Hanover (ill. 10, architects: Andrus Koresaar, Roivo Kotov, Tallinn). Photovoltaic modules cast in PC or PMMA are protected from weather and

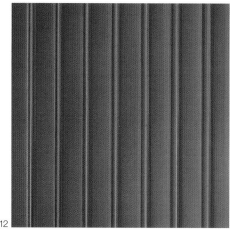

mechanical stress. GRP sheeting does not only offer the possibility of a variety of fibres and resins (ill. 11). Decorative sheeting with grasses and leaves are the preferred material of the French architect Jean de Giacinto (ill. 16).

The following design possibilities are available for finishing semi-finished products, most of which are carried out by post-processing firms:

Coating
Coatings are offered for PMMA and PC hollow cellular sheeting, which is often used to glaze conservatories in homes. The coatings break the surface tension on the sheeting and thus stop the formation of water droplets. So-called "No Drop" or "Drop-less" coatings are applied by a chemical process and stop condensation dripping inside the room, increase the self-cleaning effect by rain on the outside and prevent patches after drying, as drops of condensed water are broken down into a thin film.
Double coatings based on polysiloxane are used on solid PC sheeting to increase scratch-resistance, and abrasion and chemical resistance (graffiti removal). We will have to see in future how much nano-technological processes will be able to achieve further surface qualities like reflection reduction and easy-to-clean effects. Thermochromically coated plastics change their colour with temperature changes, photochromically coated plastics with light intensity. The most ambitious project is the planned PMMA roof planned by Santiago Calatrava for the Athens 2004 Olympic Stadium, which is intended to go darker when the sun shines on it.

Printing
Printing on transparent plastic displays used for illuminated advertising signs, and in construction for shops and exhibitions; some printed sheeting can even be swaged. But even cellular sheeting for entire facades can have print on the inside. The effect depends on the brightness and colour of the printed matter. The oversize, brightly coloured fruit motifs in the juice shop at Darmstadt station (ill. 14, architect: liquid, Darmstadt) are clearly visible even without backlighting, the black leaf structure of the Ricola warehouse building steps demurely into the background in the daytime (ill. 17 and page 39).

Painting
Many kinds of sheeting can be completely painted or provided with painted lettering.

Applying film
Microprisms on films produced by the micro-replication principle can disperse and deflect light. The optical laminated films that have recently come on to the market can produce effects in which the colours of the rainbow change according to viewing angle, thus achieving reduced heat input (ill. 12).

Filling
If hollow cellular sheeting is filled with aerogel granulate, heat transmittance can be greatly reduced – the panel functions as transparent heat insulation. The cells prevent the aerogel form settling irregularly, a problem that used to occur in filled panes of insulating glass. Cellular sheeting can also be filled for creative purposes: the facade of an internet café in London is filled with coloured liquids (architect: Blauel, London), and coffee beans decorate the walls of a Viennese coffee house (ill. 15, architect: Querkraft, Vienna).

Multi-shell structure
If different requirements cannot be met by a single product, multi-shell structure is a possible approach. Thus the inner shell of light domes can be made of impact resistant polycarbonate, and the outside of weatherproof acrylic glass. The wall of the temporary children's art gallery in the Rotterdam municipal park consists of a lightweight timber wall with transparent corrugated polycarbonate sheeting as an outer shell - the coloured effect derives from the red diffusible membrane behind (ill. 13, architects: XX-Architekten, Rotterdam).

13

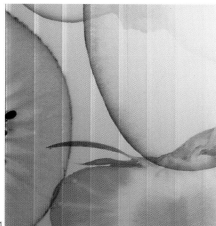
14

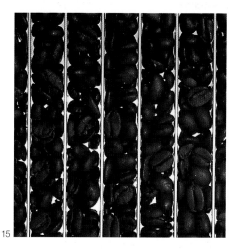
15

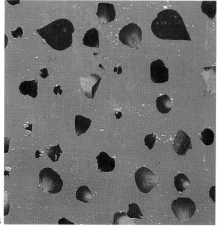
16

17

18 a   b   c
    d   e   f

The dream of free form

One key property of plastics that is not taken into account by mass products, which are usually offered in sheet form: it is very easy to shape. Cold-bending radii, which are dependent on the rigidity of the sheeting, are used only for tunnel vaults curved in one direction. But it is precisely in the field of free form that the possibilities of plastic can be extended and architecture realized that has existed for a long time on computer screens.

The facade of the Kunsthaus in Graz
The plastic cladding for Peter Cook's Kunsthaus Graz was conceived as a backlit, translucent media facade – around a closed, heat-insulated air-conditioning envelope (ill. 23). The spherically curved panels are approx. 2 x 3 m in size and mounted with point-fasteners about 30 cm away from the outer skin. The building's complex geometry means that each panel is individually tailored and curved. Because of the shape, mineral glass would have been prohibitively expensive. The open joints run along the steel support structure, which is built on a polygonal space lattice. It was important to achieve precisely the blue-green shimmering quality that the architect had prescribed. Two materials were developed further or modified to the point where they could be produced: PMMA as a thermoplastic material and GRP fibrous composite material as a thermoset.

PMMA option
The acrylic glass needed a flame-retardant additive to meet the local fire prevention requirements. A sprinkler system in the facade cavity prevents irreversible plastic distortion of the sheeting in the event of fire. PMMA sheeting is available in cast or extruded semi-finished form. Cast sheeting was selected because it is easier to shape. Extruded material is also less resistant to chemicals because of its shorter molecular chains. The specially developed tinting was achieved with blue-green colour pigments, and the slight fogging with ground polystyrene particles that were mixed into the monomer compound. Key features when planning a point-secured acrylic glass facade are the high degree of thermal expansion and sensitivity to longitudinal load. Expansion as a result of temperature changes is five times that of steel, which needs generous provision for movement in the fasteners. Given indoor and outdoor temperature differences of the kind that can occur in case of sudden summer rain, the material is prone to sudden shape changes and bulging. In the case of statically indeterminate fixing, in other words with two or more fastening points on each side, this places additional loading on the central fastening points. Because PMMA is inclined to relax, in other words to plastic distortion under constant loading, only very low continuing stresses are permitted in the design of panel and fastening. For this reason, a material thickness of 15 or 20 mm was chosen. The panels are each attached at six points. From a fixed point, the other fasteners permit free expansion of the material in all directions. A soft adhesive is used to avoid stress concentrations.

GRP option
GRP fibrous composite material was examined as a second variant. One important bonus is the availability of a B1 approved translucent material. A specimen several square metres in size was produced in a CNC-milled negative mould using the resin transfer moulding method (RTM). The coloured polyester resin is drawn into the glass fabric under a vacuum, so that no fogging air-pockets can build up. After hardening, the panels are tempered before achieving their final strength, which is many times higher than that of acrylic glass. The edge trimming and the fastener drill holes are created on the CNC machine by putting both the work and the mould back into the machine after the final hardening. If the panels are to be durable, it is important that the cut edges are sealed with resin again. This process demands a high level of technical and craft skill from the worker. Each sheet is prepared by hand, and colour fidelity is dependent on many processing factors. The material is very amenable to handling for facade purposes. Point fasteners can be screwed to the panel in the same way as in glass construction, without fear of overload. UV resistance is fully guaranteed thanks to today's gel-coat resins. The specimen panels had a very good surface and a high level of unfogged translucency. The thickness of the material was set at 8 or 10 mm.

Composite material option
In order to raise the comparatively low long-term service temperature of PMMA (e.g. when heat builds up in the facade cavity) and to be able to accommodate the loads and stresses of the fasteners with a higher modulus of elasticity, one of the tendering companies offered to lami-

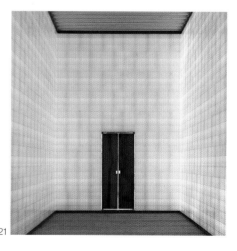

17 Ricola warehouse, Mulhouse
 Material: printed PC hollow cellular sheeting
 Architects: Herzog & de Meuron, Basel
18 Fixings
 a standard fixing with press-strip
 b–f fixing methods without press strip
19 Peace Pavilion, Venice Biennale 2000
 Material: 2-shell PMMA strips, outside 10 mm, inside 5 mm between blocks of pressed polypropylene.
 Architects: Massimiliano Fuksas, Doriana O. Mandrelli, Rome
20 House in Tokyo
 Material: 2× GRP corrugated sheets, membrane cushions filled with PE fibres (actually packing material), plastic sheeting, interior removable nylon membrane
 Architect: Shigeru Ban, Tokyo
21 Pavilion in Rotterdam
 Translucent drinks crates, special series
 Architects: Atelier Kempe Thill, Rotterdam

Plastic
The dream of free form – Everything possible in the future?

22

23

22 R129 house project
    Architects: Werner Sobek with Maren Sostmann,
    Stuttgart
23 Kunsthaus Graz
    Architects: Spacelab Cook/Fournier with
    ArchitekturConsult, Graz, Completed late 2003

Suggested literature:

Dr.- Ing. Bodo Carlowitz:
Kunststoff-Tabellen, 4. Auflage,
Carl Hanser Verlag, Munich / Vienna, 1995

Hans Domininghaus:
Die Kunststoffe und ihre Eigenschaften,
Springer Verlag, Berlin / Heidelberg, 1998

Institut für Bauen mit Kunststoffen e.V.:
Bauen mit Kunststoffen, Jahrbuch 2002,
Ernst & Sohn, Berlin, 2001

Chris Lefteri:
Kunststoff, Material-Herstellung-Producte,
avedition, Ludwigsburg, 2002

Karl Oberbach: Saechtling
Kunststoff Taschenbuch,
Carl Hanser Verlag, Munich, 1998

Prof. Dr.-Ing. Wilbrand Woebcken:
Kunststoff-Lexikon, 9. Auflage,
Carl Hanser Verlag, Munich / Vienna, 1998

nate the PMMA shells with GRP on a primer (binding layer) to make it into a composite material. The visual and technical properties were convincing, but the cost far higher than either PMMA or GRP.

PMMA outside PETG inside
Finally the choice fell on PMMA, which is unbeatable for brilliance, weather-resistance and a homogeneous surface. This decision about material was then taken into account with constructive measures like widening the joints in the upper parts of the building from 4 cm originally to 7.1 or 15 cm, for better ventilation of the facade cavity. As barely combustible materials are prescribed for the interior of the building, it was not possible to use PMMA on the underside of the "Bubble" that forms the ceiling of the children's play area. Polyester sheeting (PETG) was used in this weather-protected section. No one sheeting is like another. The geometry was applied to mould construction with specially developed software. Master and support moulds had to be produced. It will take six months for all the 1400 individual moulds, generated with the most up-to-date five axis milling centres, have been thermoformed.

Everything possible in the future?
Free form, combined with a single-shell, multi-functional plastic facade, has now become a tangible possibility as an entirely adequate building envelope in terms of building physics. The pioneers in this field are the vehicle industry and aircraft and space technology. Here plastics are increasingly pushing glass out. The Smart's complex side windows are already made of polycarbonate. Researcher are working on using plastics for windscreens coated with scratchproof silica glass.

R 129 house project
The R 129 house project by Werner Sobek Ingenieure is intended to show how far similar technologies can also be applied to architecture (ill. 22). The intention is to use acrylic glass (PMMA, polymethyl methyl acrylate) for the single-shell building envelope. This will be laminated with a layer 1 mm thick of chemically tempered glass, making it guaranteed scratch-proof and resistant to chemicals. An internal low-E coating is intended to prevent heat radiation outwards in winter and inwards in summer. An application of controllable electrochromic film means that the envelope can be darkened in part, or made completely transparent.
The jointing technique is also unusual for a heat-insulated facade. The PMMA elements are to be glued together and function as a self-supporting shell without clamping elements or a secondary support structure - changes of length mean that the apex of the spherical surface rises and falls. Something that still sounds utopian today will be complete and a concrete presence in a few years.

Membrane

Membrane materials in structural engineering – Meshes and films

Karsten Moritz

The concept of the membrane goes back to the Latin word "membrana", which can be translated as skin or parchment. The characteristic of these two materials is that they are both thin. This also applies to modern membranes. If they are used to disperse loads, they have to be additionally tensionable, and able to adopt a curved shape in a space. As a mechanically pre-tensioned structure they ideally form an area that is doubled in the space and curved in the opposite direction, while pneumatically pre-tensioned systems show double curvature in the same direction in wide areas. Modern membranes used in building construction as load-transmitting surfaces have to be capable of being tensioned and adopting three-dimensionally curved forms. The thin skin is able to resist only tension loads. Mechanically tensioned membranes should ideally form a doubly counter-curved surface; while pneumatically tensioned systems are usually in the form of doubly curved surfaces in a single direction.

Only in this way can the membrane resist opposing forces, such as wind suction, wind pressure and snow loading, and transmit them economically and safely to the primary structure and the foundations. Since the 1950s, the development of plastics technology – especially in the form of composite materials – has led to increasing numbers of innovative membrane projects. Materials of great strength now allow the construction of large-span, translucent roof structures with slender dimensions and without intermediate columns. In the future, one may expect an ever greater use of membrane systems as permanent space-enclosing structures, even under the climatic conditions prevailing in central and northern Europe.

Membrane materials

The products used for membranes may be divided into two main groups in terms of their load-bearing properties: anisotropic materials, and those that at least approximate to an isotropic state. The latter have identical mechanical properties in all directions and, where used in building construction, generally consist of thin thermoplastic skins or, more rarely, metallic sheeting. Metallic sheeting is not further discussed here because it is so rarely used in building. (for this see [5]). Anisotropic membranes are usually in the form of technical textiles of various kinds. These fabrics may be divided into three main types, according to the nature of their manufacture:

- mesh fabrics (knitted)
- woven fabric
- the so-called "non-wovens" (fleece, felt, layered fibres, etc.).

Woven fabrics have mechanical properties that make them particularly suitable for use as a load-dispersing material for textile membranes.[6] As system is designated woven – at least in a tensioned state – if it exhibits a more or less orthogonal thread structure, each of the threads usually consisting of several hundred individual fibres.[3]
The following fibres might be used

- natural fibres
- mineral fibres
- metallic fibres
- synthetic fibres

If the fibres are made synthetically, and are thus effectively endless, then the threads made from them are known as filaments. If the thread is made of a single synthetic fibre, it is known as a monofilament. Synthetic fibres can be produced to various cross-sections, which may be matched to specific requirements. Natural fibres (e.g. cotton, silk, hemp or flax) are usually roughly circular in section, and their diameter and length cannot be varied. The diameter of a natural fibre is usually larger than 0.1 mm, while synthetic fibres can also be thinner.[6] Since the slenderness of a fibre makes it difficult to determine its exact cross-section, the process of calculating the precise tensions in a fabric is extremely complicated. In accordance with German standards, the unit N/5cm (instead of N/mm^2) has now established itself as a means of describing the strength of fabrics used in membrane construction, according to DIN 53 354.

In the textile industry, a filament yarn is described according to its length-related mass (fineness), the number of its filaments and details about the twists of the filaments per metre. The unit of fineness is the "tex" = weight in grams per 1000 m length. Figures are more usually given in decitex, "dtex" for short = weight in grams per 10,000 m length. A yarn defined as 1100 dtex f 200 z 60 weighs 1100 g per 10,000 m and is made up of 200 filaments, twisted together 60 times per metres to the right over the axis of the yarn (z direction).

1   Japanese Pavilion EXPO 2000, Hanover
    External material:
    Polyester fabric, PVC-coated
    five internal layers:
    polyethylene sheeting, flame resistant
    non-combustible paper
    glass-fibre fabric
    non-combustible paper
    polyethylene sheeting, flame resistant
    Architect: Shigeru Ban Architects, Tokyo
    Structural engineers: Büro Happold, Berlin
    Structural consultant: Frei Otto, Warmbronn

As an initial measure of whether a fibrous material is appropriate for use in large-span structures, the free tearing length can be used. This strikingly describes the relationship between the weight and the tensile strength of a material; i.e. the length in kilometres at which an unstretched thread suspended at one end will tear under its own weight. The approximate tearing length of steel, for example, is 25 km, of cotton 48 km, polyamide (nylon) 89 km, polyester 94 km, glass 140 km, carbon 153 km and aramide 190 km.[6]

The threads in the direction in which the fabric is manufactured are referred to as the warp, those at right angles to this are the weft.

There are three basic eaves, dependent on the handling of warp and weft:

• plain weave
• twill weave
• satin weave

There are also various sub-types of weave, of which the basket weave (one warp thread/one weft thread) or the Panama weave (2/2 or 3/3) are most common in membranes for tent structures, because their seams are stronger. The way the crossing threads are woven leads to a characteristic waviness in the threads included.

Since the warp threads are prestressed during the manufacturing process, they will usually have a less wavy form, a greater stiffness and a smaller breaking elongation than the weft threads. These different mechanical properties can be controlled in the weaving process and exploited for construction. The weave is the key to all this, but other characteristics of the fabric, such as tearing strength and buckling resistance, can be affected by surface coatings and seals. Coating also prevents angular twisting and thus enhances the shearing rigidity of the membrane when under short-term load.

2 Airship hangar, Briesen-Brand
   Material: polyester fabric, PVC-coated
   Architects: SIAT Architekten + Technik, Munich
   Structural engineers: Ove Arup & Partner, Düsseldorf
   Membrane design and planning:
   IPL, Ingenieurplanung und Leichtbau, Radolfzell
   Membrane construction:
   Birdair Europe Stromeyer, Konstanz
3 Daylight diffusion wings, DaimlerChrysler Design Center, Sindelfingen
   Material: EFTE fabric, THV-coated
   Architects: Renzo Piano Building Workshop, Genoa
   Membrane construction: Aeronautec, Chieming

2

Surface coatings

Coatings, usually applied to both faces, protect the membrane against moisture, UV radiation, fire, and microbe and fungus attack. They also influence the resistance to soiling and the life of a fabric, and sometimes its fire resistance as well. Coatings are a permanent means of waterproofing the fabric, and they can facilitate a controlled coloration of the membrane in the form of surface printing or through the addition of pigments. Since the fabric threads cannot usually be joined together directly, coatings also allow areas of a membrane to be jointed by means of thermal or high-frequency welding. The corollary of this is that uncoated fabrics normally have to be joined with sewn seams. The two main exceptions are uncoated fluoropolymer fabrics – the threads of which can be welded – and silicone coatings, which are joined exclusively with adhesives. Today, the most common coatings are polyvinyl chloride (PVC), polytetrafluoroethylene (PTFE) and silicone. PTFE coatings can be used only with fabrics whose fibres have a melting point above that of PTFE (roughly 327 °C), such as glass. That is why PTFE cannot be used as a coating for polyester fabrics (melting temperature 220–260 °C). Other coating materials available for special situations include THV, PVDF, acrylic esters, polyurethane and rubber, although they are, in fact, rarely used.

Whereas PTFE and silicone show no significant signs of ageing – becoming brittle, cracking or abrasion – over a period of at least 25 to 30 years, PVC is sensitive to weathering. To make it elastic, various additives are required, such as plasticizers (roughly 40 per cent by weight). Small quantities of UV and heat stabilizers are also necessary. In addition, PVC should be protected, at least on the outer face, by a sealing layer (topcoating). The impermeability of this seal to vapour minimizes the escape and dissipation of the material components. It also reduces the UV radiation acting on the coating layer and thus prevents the long-term breakdown of the PVC polymer structure. Moreover, after sealing, the surface will be smooth and non-adhesive, which greatly enhances the non-soiling properties of the material.

In the early days, PVC-coated fabrics were inadequately sealed, with the result that they became brittle within a relatively short time and developed cracks, which in turn allowed the penetration of dirt and microbes. Today, the acrylic and PVDF

coatings and PVF laminates that are commonly used for sealing purposes provide a durable, efficient form of protection. The disadvantage of PVDF coatings is their high melting point. This means that prior to making up the membrane, the coating has to be removed in the areas of welded seams without damaging the fabric. PVF laminates, with a thickness of roughly 25 µm, provide the best protection, but they are also expensive. They have to be removed before the fabric can be welded, and they result in a reduced buckling resistance of the membrane, which is why they are not suitable for structures that have to be modified or transported. PTFE coatings also have a topcoat. This usually consists of FEP or PFA fluorine plastics, which improve anti-adhesive properties, the mechanical properties of the surface and weldability. In regions with a humid climate, fungicidal coatings are used to prevent attack by mould.

Requirements and applications

Parallel to the development of new materials, questions of recycling are likely to assume an increasingly important role in the specification of membrane structures in the future. This applies in particular to composite materials. To determine the range of applications, quantifiable data on the following aspects will be necessary: fire protection; thermal and acoustic insulation; the mechanical properties of the material and appropriate jointing techniques; its weight per unit area; manufacturing dimensions; surface texture and scope for coloration; resistance to soiling/ ease of cleaning; permeability to vapour and moisture; transmission, absorption and reflection in the infrared, ultraviolet and visible spectra; and resistance to chemical and biological substances (including salts, acids, fungi and bacteria) as well as to mechanical abrasion (hail, vandalism, etc.). In this context, it should not be forgotten that the properties of materials can vary within the relevant temperature range and during the estimated life of the membrane. In large-scale projects, the availability of adequate quantities of the fabric, as well as the necessary periods for planning and assembly, will all play a role. Last, but not least, the economic viability of the structure and its appearance will be of central importance. Any comparison of the costs of membrane construction and traditional forms of building should take account of the fact that the use of membranes has to be planned in conjunction with the load-bearing structure. In other words, the entire building will

3

Membranes
Requirements and applications

4 Carport, Amt für Abfallwirtschaft, Munich
Material: glass-fibre fabric, PTFE-coated
Architects: Ackermann und Partner, Munich
Structural engineers: Schlaich, Bergermann und Partner, Stuttgart
Membrane design and dimensions: Tensys, Bath
Membrane construction:
Birdair Europe Stromeyer, Konstanz
5 Carport, Amt für Abfallwirtschaft, Munich

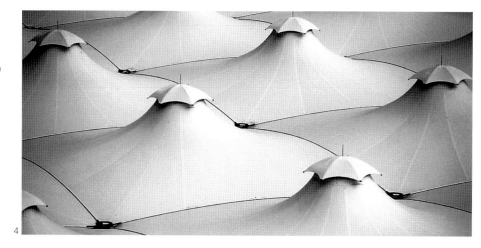
4

Suggested literature:

[1] Baier, B.: Neue Entwicklungsansätze und Ziele im Membranbau. In: Baukultur, issue 2, 1999
[2] Moritz, Karsten: Materialeinsatz und Konfektionierung von Membranwerkstoffen. In: Stahlbau, issue 8, 2000
[3] Orpana, M.; Houtman, R.: Materials for Membrane Structures, Beitrag zum Workshop "Textile Roofs", Berlin 2000
[4] Pawlowski, R.: Definition der Membran, Seminar Membranbauwerke, Universität Stuttgart, Institut für Baukonstruktion, 1994
[5] Schlaich, J.; Greiner, S.: Vorgespannte Flächentragwerke aus Metallmembranen. In: Bauingenieur 53 (1978), pp. 77–87
[6] Sobek, Werner; Speth, Martin: Textile Werkstoffe. In: Bauingenieur 70 (1995), pp. 243–250
[7] Tritthardt, J.; Ayrle, H.: Textile Fassadensysteme. In: Baukultur, issue 2, 1999

further:

Baier, Bernd (ed.): Skelett und Haut, Symposium, Fachgebiet Konstruktive Gestaltung, Leichtbau, Fachbereich 10 – Bauwesen, Universität GH Essen. 1998

Baier, Bernd (ed.): Leicht Bau Kunst, Symposium, Fachgebiet Konstruktive Gestaltung, Leichtbau, Fachbereich 10 – Bauwesen, Universität GH Essen. 2001

Barnes, Michael; Dickson, Michael: Widespan Roof Structures. Thomas Telford. 2000

Berger, Horst: Light Structures, Structures of Light – The Art and Engineering of Tensile Architecture. Basel: Birkhäuser Verlag. 1996

Brinkmann, Günther (ed.): DFG Deutsche Forschungsgemeinschaft – Leicht und Weit – Zur Konstruktion weitgespannter Flächentragwerke – Ergebnisse aus dem Sonderforschungsbereich 64 "Weitgespannte Flächentragwerke", Universität Stuttgart. Weinheim: VCH Verlag

Bubner, Ewald: Membrankonstruktionen – Verbindungstechniken. Essen: Druckerei Wehlmann GmbH. 1997

Ishii, Kazuo (ed.): Structural Design of Retractable Roof Structures, Southampton: WIT Press. 2000

Ishii, Kazuo (ed.): Membrane Designs and Structures in the World. Tokyo: Shinkenchiku-sha Co., Ltd. 1999
Mitteilungen des Instituts für leichte Flächentragwerke (IL, heute ILEK). Universität Stuttgart

Otto, Frei; Rasch, Bodo: Gestalt finden – Auf dem Weg zu einer Baukunst des Minimalen. Edition Axel Menges. 1995

Scheuermann, Rudi; Boxer, Keith: Tensile Architecture in the Urban Context. Oxford: Butterworth-Heinemann. 1996

Schock, Hans-Joachim: Segel, Folien und Membranen. Basel: Birkhäuser Verlag. 1997

have to be taken into consideration. The simple alternative of a sheet metal or glass-roof covering on the one hand and a membrane on the other is unlikely to provide a realistic comparison. The choice of a membrane structure is obviously not appropriate in all situations. The advantages of fabric forms of construction lie in their translucence or transparency, and in their greater UV transmission coefficient in comparison with glass, for which reason they are often used for palm houses and swimming baths. In certain cases, the shorter assembly times for membrane structures may prove decisive; for example, in designing exhibition buildings. This was particularly apparent in the run-up to EXPO 2000. Coverings for stands in many sporting and other arenas are a further illustration of the advantages of membrane construction, which may be largely free of columns. Variable, movable roof systems would be inconceivable without membrane materials. Although thin membranes do not generally provide adequate thermal and sound insulation, multi-layer membrane systems can be made to meet thermal insulation requirements in summer and in winter. U-values of 2.7 to 0.8 W/m²K can readily be achieved. [1] (The k-value was used in these calculations. It has now been replaced by the U-value.)
Building multi-layered membrane structures providing thermal and acoustic insulation is also now a reality. Providing adequate thermal insulation for a roof without loss of translucence, or indeed transparency, has hitherto been possible only in pneumatically supported multi-layer membranes. Membrane construction will take a further step forward with the development of multi-layer fabric systems in combination with other technologies, such as transparent thermal insulation, or installations that exploit solar energy.

The materials presented below are just a selection of the membranes available. Because plastics technology is developing so rapidly, sheets, fabrics and their coatings and seals are in a constant state of change. This applies above all in the field of fluoropolymers, whose versatility means we can expect more membranes with interesting applications in future.

5

Membranes
Material qualities

woven material (not including latticed fabrics)	material type	weight per unit area [g/m²] according to DIN 55 352	minimum tensile strength values fabric [N/ 5 cm] warp/weft according to DIN 53 354 or DIN EN ISO 527	fracture strain fabric (%) warp/weft according to DIN 53 354 or DIN EN ISO 527	tear resistance fabric [N] warp/weft according to DIN 53 363	buckling resistance
cotton fabric		350 520	1,700/1,000 2,500/2,000	35/18 38/20	60 80	very good
PTFE fabric		300 520 710	2,390/2,210 3,290/3,370 4,470/4,510	11/10 11/10 18/9	approx. 500/500	very good
ETFE fabric THV coated		250	1,200/1,200			very good
polyester fabric PVC coated	type I type II type III type IV type V	800 900 1,050 1,300 1,450	3,000/3,000 4,400/3,950 5,750/5,100 7,450/6,400 9,800/8,300	15/20 15/20 15/25 15/30 20/30	350/310 to 1,800/1,600 580/520 800/950 1,400/1,100 1,800/1,600	very good
glass-fibre fabric PTFE coated		800 1,150 1,550	3,500/3,500 5,800/5,800 7,500/6,500	7/10 to 2/17 500/500	300/300 to 500/500	adequate
glass-fibre fabric Silicone coated		800 1,270	3,500/3,000 6,600/6,000	7/10 to 2/17	300 570	adequate
aramide fibre fabric PVC coated		900 2,020	7,000/9,000 24,500/24,500	5/6	700 4,450	good
aramide fibre fabric PTFE coated		project-related	project-related, limited adjustment	project-related, limited adjustment	project-related, limited adjustment	good

sheet material	material type	weight per unit area [g/m²] according to DIN 55 352	minimum tensile strength values sheeting [N/5 cm] warp/weft according to DIN 53 354 or DIN EN ISO 527	elongation failure sheeting [%] according to DIN 53 455 or DIN EN ISO 527	tear growth resistance sheeting [N/mm] warp/weft according to DIN 53 363	buckling resistance
ETFE sheeting	50 µm 80 µm 100 µm 150 µm 200 µm	87.5 140 175 262.5 350	64/56 58/54 58/57 58/57 52/52	450/500 500/600 550/600 600/650 600/600	450/450 450/450 430/440 450/430 430/430	satisfactory
THV sheeting	500 µm	980	22/21	540/560	255/250	good
PVC sheeting						satisfactory

UV resistance	achievable building class according to DIN 4102	translucency [%]	useful life (a)	standard colours	frequent uses
adequate	B2	varies	< 5	large selection of colours on request	temporary, mobile, adaptable, permanent structures, small span
very good	A2	to approx. 37	> 25	standard white, other colours on request	adaptable structures, especially for screening structures
very good	B1	to approx. 90	> 25	standard white and natural, other colours on request	indoor uses, also outdoors with load restriction
good	B1	to approx. 4.0	> 20	standard white, wide range of colours on request	temporary, mobile, adaptable, permanent structures, standard systems
very good	A 2	to approx. 13	> 25	standard white, limited range of colours on request	permanent structures, standard systems, not adaptable
very good	A2	to approx. 25	> 20	standard white, limited range of colours on request	permanent structures, not adaptable
adequate	B1	none in principle	> 20	standard white, wide range of colours on request	permanent structures, large spans, not translucent, not adaptable
adequate	A2	none in principle	> 25	standard white, limited range of colours on request	permanent structures, large spans, not translucent, not adaptable
UV resistance	achievable building class according to DIN 4102	translucency [%]	useful life (a)	standard colours	frequent uses
very good	B1	to approx. 95	> 25	standard transparent white or blue, other colours or printing on request	zoo buildings greenhouses swimming baths façades and atriums
good	B1	to approx. 95	> 20	standard transparent, other colours on request	indoor use outdoor use small spans
adequate	B1	to approx. 95	< 5	various standard colours	indoor use

Cotton fabrics

Cotton and mixed-fibre fabrics containing cotton are usually not coated, but impregnated. Impregnation lends the material a fire-resistant, fungicidal and water-repellent surface for a time. In the relevant temperature range, cotton is also resistant to heat and normal concentrations of chemicals. Mixed-fibre fabrics usually consist of 25–50 % cotton and 50–75 % polyester.[4]

Because of their organic content, both kinds are used in textile construction only indoors or for temporary structures subject to minimal loading. This is above all because of their lower strength (cotton: max. ca. 1,500 N/5 cm), their lower elasticity and shorter life – despite impregnation – when exposed to weathering in the open air (up to about 5 years).[7] Factors influencing the behaviour of the fabric include the dead or unripe cotton fibre content.[4]

Unlike those made of natural fibres, fabrics consisting exclusively of mineral (glass) or synthetically manufactured fibres (e.g. polyester or aramide) achieve 6 to 15 times more breaking strength and a 4 to 5 times higher life expectancy.

Ill. impregnated, permeable cotton fabric.

Metal fabrics

Woven metal fabrics are permeable and usually consist of round, flat or stranded wires, or cables in stainless steel, titanium-, chromium- or chromium-nickel-steel (sometimes in non-ferrous metals, too). Round wires have standard diameters of between 18 μm and 16 mm. According to fibre and thread of a textile weave, a braid is produced by tripling at least 3 and at most 9 wires.

The standard core diameter of the braid is between 100 and 800 μ. A cable is tripled from at least 3 and most 9 braids. With an individual wire diameter of over 3 mm the wave line of the wires is pre-shaped, but it is difficult to apply pre-tension – dependent on the wave-line – to these undulating grilles.

Of the various weaves used, the most common is the basket weave, though the twill weave is also used for metal fabrics (and sometimes even the satin weave). In the twill weave, at least two wires are tied in pair by pair. At present, woven metal fabrics are available with a standard sheet width of 6 m (up to 8 m in special cases). A wide range of surface textures can be achieved by means of pickling, anodizing, painting, etc. Woven metal fabrics are used for facade cladding, soffits, aviaries, as sunshading, for electromagnetic protection and as a safety device against burglary. For metal weaves see also p. 80 ff.

Ill.: permeable metal weave, uncoated.

Fluoropolymer fabrics

Uncoated fluopolymer fabrics are usually manufactured in mono-filament form. The most important fluoropolymer fabric at present is PTFE. Its market share in textile construction is low, given the high price of the material and its excellent creep and relaxation properties (strength approx. 4,500 N/5 cm and a weight of 710 g/m^2). As a non-combustible material, PTFE fabric can meet DIN 4102-A2 requirements. Depending on the nature and thickness of the material, its light transmission rate can be up to 37 %.

It also possesses excellent resistance to soiling, abrasion and buckling so is often used for movable sunshading systems. Since there are examples of fluoropolymer sheeting that are more than 25 years old and that show no serious signs of ageing, a similar life may be expected for the fabric. In view of the open weave, however, uncoated fabrics may be subject to attack from dirt, moisture, biological and chemical substances.

It is advantageous here to apply a full fluoropolymer coating, e.g. THV (a terpolymer consisting of TFE, HFP and VDF units).

Ill.: uncoated, permeable PTFE fabric.

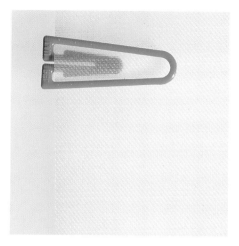

Fluoropolymer fabrics
The main types presently used in membrane building include:

- PTFE (polytetrafluoroethylene)
- ETFE (ethylene-tetrafluorethylene)
- TFA/PFA (tetrafluoroethylene perflouoroalkylvinyl ether or perfluoride co-components)
- TFE, HFP and VDF co-polymer, THV for short
- FEP (tetrafluoroethylene-hexafluoropropylene)
- PVDF (polyvinyl fluoride)

The individual fluoropolymer combinations are better known by their trade names, such as Teflon, Hostaflon, Polyflon, Toyoflon or Tedlar.
Because of their strong bond, they are extremely resistant to chemical and biological attack as well as to long-term exposure to the weather and UV radiation.
Coatings are, therefore, not necessary as a means of preserving the fabric, but they may be required to create a watertight surface.
Coated fluoropolymer fabrics, like for example THV-coated PTFE or ETFE fabrics, or also PVDF-coated PVDF fabrics can consist of a combination of two different fluoropolymer substances for the fabric and the coating.
In view of the maximum breaking strength of coated fluoropolymer membranes (approx. 1,200 N/5 cm), their weight (250 g/m²) and the low strength of welded seams, the use of this material is limited to small spans or internal situations.

The material is permeable to diffuse (low-glare) light in the daylight spectrum, which results in pleasant indoor conditions. The permeability to light of the THV-coated ETFE fabric is up to 90 %, a value that cannot be achieved with any other fully coated membrane. In the years to come, these membrane systems will presumably also be complemented by a number of additional fluoropolymer combinations, which could ultimately open up a new and interesting range of applications. The fact that coated fluoropolymer fabrics lend themselves to many material combinations and can be easily modified, means that they have a great potential in the field of membrane structures.
Ill. top left: fluoropolymer-coated fluoropolymer fabric
Ill. top centre: PVC-coated polyester fabric

PVC-coated polyester fabrics
PVC-coated polyester fabrics, usually called PVC/PES fabric, are among the most commonly used materials for membrane structures because of their material properties and reasonable price.
Their great potential strength (type 5 up to 9,800 N/5 cm), their tearing strength (up to 1,800 N) and their high elasticity (breaking elongation up to approx. 30 %) make them suitable for large-span planar bearing structures. Their translucence is usually between about 0.8 % and 4 % or even higher in the case of permeable latticed fabrics, though at the expense of strength.
As flameproof materials, PVC-coated polyester fabrics are usually in fire class DIN 4102-B1, and – like all membranes – because of their low weight (up to about 1,450 g/m²) and with a maximum thickness of about 1.2 mm, they have an extremely low fire load. The fabric melts in a fire, thus creating the possibility of extracting heat and smoke directly.
Surface seals provide the coating with long-term protection against soiling and against premature ageing, so that as a rule, these fabrics have a life of more than 20 years. They are used across the whole range of textile construction.
Ill.: permeable, PVC-coated polyester latticed material

PTFE-coated glass-fibre fabrics
PTFE-coated glass-fibre fabrics have matured to be a high-quality material with a life of at least 25 to 30 years, and have come to be seen as a standard product in textile construction.

The fabric consists of glass filament yarns of different diameter (approx. 4 µm, 6 µm, 9 µm etc). Because the glass fabric has been impregnated, no moisture can penetrate the gaps in the fabric, which also almost completely excludes penetration by particles of dirt, microbes or fungal spores. Only liquids with a low surface tension, gases and vapours can penetrate the microporous PTFE coating. The strengths in the case of a heavy standard type, at 7500 N/5 cm are less than the strongest standard PVC-coated polyester fabric type. The material yield (breaking elongation approx. 3 % to 10 %) and tearing strength (up to approx. 500 N) are low because of the relatively brittle glass fabric.

Completely coated PTFE glass fibre fabrics can achieve up to 13 % translucency, and as permeable or non-permeable latticed fabrics up to approx. 65 % – but at the expense of strength.

They are classed as non-combustible materials under DIN 4102-A2. Because of their relatively low buckling strength they are not suitable for use in situations involving change (folding) or mobility.
Ill.: PTFE-coated, non-permeable glass fibre fabric

Silicone-coated glass-fibre fabrics
These fabrics were rarely used in building in the past, because they are easily charged with static electricity and attract dirt. They have similar mechanical properties to PTFE-coated glass-fibre membranes, since they have the same load-transmitting fabric base. The main differences lie in the coating.

For example, silicone, which is not vapour diffusing, provides better protection than microporous PTFE. Furthermore, the combination of silicone and glass fibre results in a far better degree of translucence (over 20 %). Silicone-coated glass-fibre fabrics can also reach the DIN 4102-A2 class.

Since silicone cannot be thermally welded, the individual membrane segments are joined with adhesive to create strong, permanent connections. But in recent years, its anti-soiling and behaviour and connecting techniques have improved, so that silicone-coated glass-fibre membranes – more reasonably priced than PTFE-coated material – have become standard in the building world.
Ill.: silicone-coated, non-permeable glass-fibre fabric.

PVC-coated aramide-fibre fabrics
With a breaking elongation of 5–6 %, PVC-coated aramide-fibre fabrics can have a maximum failing strength of roughly 24,500 N/5 cm. They are, therefore, the strongest of the synthetic fabric membranes.

Aramide is an abbreviation of aromatic polyamide. The even, strong chemical bonding of these materials results in a relatively stiff fibre that is resistant to chemical and thermal influences. Since it is not resistant to UV radiation, though, the fabric has to be completely covered with an opaque PVC (or PTFE) coating.

According to the nature and scope of the coating, PVC-coated aramide-fibre fabrics are fame-resistant, and fall in to fire class DIN 4102-B1, and DIN 4102-A2 with PTFE coating. For a heavy material type, the breaking strength of PVC-coated aramide-fibre fabrics is also very high: 4,450 N at 2020 g/m².

The use of PVC-coated aramide-fibre fabrics will probably continue to be restricted to situations where great strength is required, but where elasticity and translucence are less important.
Ill.: PVC-coated, non-permeable polyester latticed fabric.

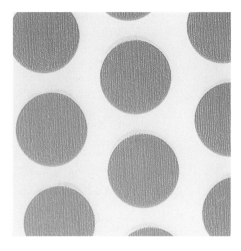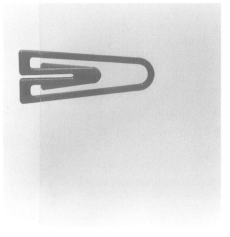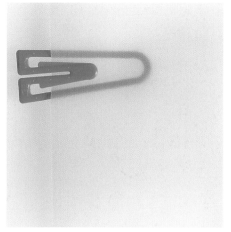

Synthetic sheeting or film
Isotropic film or sheeting exhibits a ten-sion-stretching behaviour that is virtually equal in all directions, unlike anisotropic fabrics. Of the many kinds of synthetic sheeting that are available, two groups of thermoplastic materials are of special importance in membrane construction. These are fluoropolymer sheeting (mainly ETFE and THV) and polyvinylchloride sheeting (PVC).

ETFE sheeting
Generally speaking, the same criteria apply to fluoropolymer sheeting as to fluoropolymer fabrics. In view of its excel-lent mechanical properties, its stability and the good fire-resistance (DIN 4102-B1) it can achieve, ETFE sheeting is the material most commonly used for pneumatically supported membrane structures. Standard thicknesses are between 0.05 and 0.20 mm. Coloured sheets can be produced by the addition of pigments; alternatively, the membrane can be given a printed surface. Since the tearing strength of the strongest standard material (0.25 mm = 250 µm) at some-thing over 653 N/5cm is considerably less than that of a type 1 PVC-coated polyes-ter fabric (3000 N/5 cm), the maximum spans of external load-transmitting mem-brane structures in ETFE sheeting are much smaller than those that can be achieved with coated fabrics.
The estimated life of ETFE film is at least 25–30 years. The strips, usually manufac-tured by broad-slit extrusion, have a max-imum width of 1.55 m. One advantage of ETFE sheeting over glass is that with a light-transmission rate of roughly 95 % per layer (200µm), transparent ETFE sheeting has an extremely high permea-bility to UV radiation and is increasingly used for the roofs of palm houses, green-houses, swimming baths, etc.
For ETFE sheeting see p. 70 ff.

THV sheeting
THV sheeting is transparent and as resil-ient as ETFE; and it can also be used in outdoor locations. It has a lower tearing strength, however, and is not suitable for large-span load-bearing structures. It is made in thicknesses from 0.08 mm to several millimetres and in standard widths of 500–1,500 mm.
Ill. left: EFTE sheeting with printed dot pattern
Ill. centre: transparent EFTE sheeting

Polyvinyl chloride sheeting (PVC)
PVC sheeting is of extremely low strength and great ductility. In addition, it has a low resistance to UV radiation and heat. It is, therefore, used exclusively indoors. PVC sheeting has good fire-resisting properties (DIN 4102 B1) and can be supplied transparent (approx. 95 % light transmission), coloured or of a milky obscured quality, with approx. 79 % light transmission. It is therefor suited to a vari-ety of purposes: in exhibition construc-tion, for projection screens and in lighting soffits.
Ill.: milky PVC sheeting

Building with ETFE sheeting

Karsten Moritz
Rainer Barthel

The plastic sheeting used in construction today makes it possible to build envelopes that cannot be surpassed by any other material for their light and UV transmittance. These wafer-thin, transparent membranes are tension-stressed only, and reduce the weight of the outer skin and load-bearing system to a minimum. The fluoropolymer material ethylene tetrafluoroethylene, known for short was EFTE or just ET, has proved particularly suitable for this purpose. The following qualities make its preferable to other materials:

- its extremely low dead weight (350 g/m^2 at a thickness of 200 µm),
- high light and UV transmittance,
- high chemical resistance to acids and alkalis,
- a relatively long useful life (no significant changes in mechanical or visual properties have been noticed in over 20 years of practical use),
- and almost complete recyclability

make fluoropolymer sheeting an economical and environment-friendly product.

Construction principles

Thin sheeting has to be pre-tensioned if it is to be able to disperse external loads in various directions through tension forces alone, without forming folds. Two construction methods are distinguished here: pneumatically pre-stressed or supported structures, and mechanically pre-stressed structures.

Pneumatically pre-stressed structures
Although the principle of pneumatic stabilization has been known for centuries, pneumatic constructions were not used in the building industry until the second half of the 20th century. Only then did it become possible to develop plastics that were flexible, loadable and sufficiently impermeable to gas to allow major deformation, the requisite pre-tensioning and a permanent pressure difference. In the seventies composite materials still led the field, above all PVC-coated polyester fabrics. Transparent inflatables that could be used as long-lasting external envelopes were not a feasible proposition until the fluoropolymers were developed, especially EFTE sheeting. This was first used in the seventies as an enveloped for greenhouses, because of its high transmittance in the UV spectrum. From the early 80s, the material was also used for inflatable external envelope structures. These consist of at least two layers of

sheeting. Blowing creates a slight excess of pressure in the gap, which makes the sheeting into a cushion, so it is pre-stressed and stabilized. The pressure needed for stabilization is generally only approx. 200 to 1000 Pascal (Pa), which corresponds to a surface load of 0.2 to 1.0 kN/m^2, or a water column of 2 to 10 cm. The rise in the cushion caused by the pressure, in other words the maximum deviation of the lower or the upper sheet from the zero line, is usually approx. 10 to 15 % of the span width.

In rare cases, pressure is reduced rather than increased, which also provides the necessary stabilization. The limited loadability of the sheeting means that the maximum inflatable span, according to the inflatable and the roof geometry, is approx. 4.5 m for longitudinal and approx. 7.5 m for round or square inflatables. Larger spans usually need additional support from cables or cable-nets. The most frequent examples of inflatable constructions in EFTE sheeting are buildings for botanical or zoological gardens, and also for baths. In the predator house in the zoo at Hellabrunn in Munich (ill. 14), the inflatables are arranged between a pre-tensioned cable-net, which creates a double, counter-curved overall shape, which is atypical or anti-classical for inflatable structures. An impressive example is the "Eden project" (ills. 1, 3, 4, 15) in England. The domes of the building are of different sizes, with spans of approx. 38 to 125 m; they are made of ETFE sheeting inflatables, partially supported by a cable-net. The Masoala rainforest house in Zurich zoo (ill. 7) has an arched roof whose inflatables have a span of approx. 4 m and are up to 106 m long, which presumably makes them the longest inflatables in the world. A fine example of the use of EFTE sheeting for baths construction is the modernized "Moby Dick" leisure pool in Rülzheim (ill. 2). For the "Earth Centre" in England, EFTE cushions were used as modular facade elements (ill. 8).

1 Eden Project, St. Austell, Cornwall, UK
   Architects: Grimshaw & Partners, London
   Structural engineers: Anthony Hunt, Cirencester
   Membrane installation: Foiltec, Bremen

1

Mechanically pre-tensioned structures
Unlike multi-layered, pneumatically supported structures, pre-tensioned by air pressure differences, here the smaller-cut, single-layer membranes are pulled to the edges and fastened. Thus they are mechanically pre-tensioned. Mechanically tensioned ETFE sheeting has only been in use since the 1990s. Because of sheeting's low load-bearing capacity in comparison with fabric membranes [4], uses have been restricted so far to relatively small elements or to large areas with frequent support (up to approx. 1.5 m).

For the Walchensee power station information centre, which was built in this way, an ETFE membrane of about 390 m² was prepared as a piece and mechanically pre-tensioned (ills. 5, 6).

The Deutsche Budesstiftung Umwelt's environmental communications centre in Osnabrück (ill. 16) was also covered with a single-layer ETFE sheeting roof in 2002. The light coming into the rooms through the transparent, back-ventilated roof can be controlled by adjustable sunshading louvres.

Manufacture and processing
The process of making ETFE and processing it as a membrane can be broken down into four essential production steps: polymerization, granulation, extrusion and preparation. Polymerization (multiplication) means arranging small molecules (monomers) to form a large molecule. [2] A polymer is made up of the same monomers, different monomers produce a co-polymer. The ETFE polymer consists of about 25 % ethylene and 75 % tetra-fluoroethylene monomer units. [2] After polymerization, the ETFE is in powder form, and then heated (melting temperature approx. 265 °C to 285 °C) to produce granules. The granulate is then calendered or extruded to make a semi-finished material, in other words rolled sheeting. A distinction is made between blown sheeting and flat or cast sheeting according to the extruder tool used. [5] At present flat sheeting produced by the broad-slit extrusion process at a density of 1.75 g/cm³ is used exclusively in the building industry, because of its better material qualities.

Sheeting can currently be made up to 250 μm thick, with a roll width of 1.55 m. [6] At the time of writing, there are two such flat ETFE sheetings on the German

2 "Moby Dick" leisure pool, Rülzheim
Architects: Schick und Partner, Karlsruhe
Structural engineers, timber:
Ingenieurbüro Schlechter, Albstadt
Structural engineers, membrane:
Engineering + Design, Rosenheim
Membrane installation: Covertex, Obing
3 Eden Project, St. Austell, Cornwall, UK
4 Eden Project, St. Austell, Cornwall, UK
Detail of pneumatic pre-tension, scale: 1:10
1 ETFE sheeting cushions, triple layer:
internal sheeting 0.1 mm,
external sheeting 0.2 mm
2 aperture clamping unit,
extruded aluminium

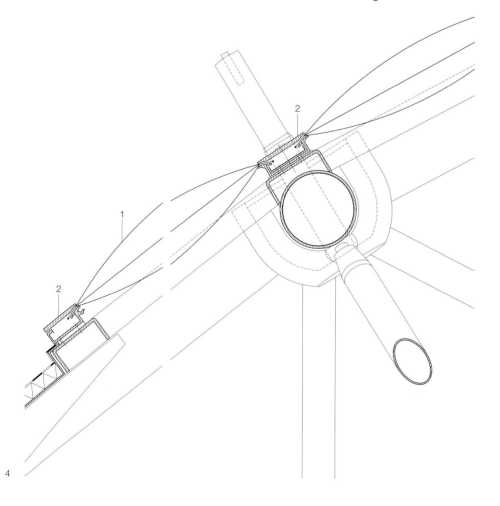

market (TOYOFLON®, NOWOFLON® or
HOSTAFLON®). Both are have test certificate ratings of DIN EN 10204 para. 2.2.
This implies key ratings and manufacturing tolerances based on non-specific
tests by the manufacturer – following
official standards and regulations. So far
only a few companies are able to pre-
weld the rolled material to form curved
membrane to tailored specifications, in
other words to prepare it. In welding a
distinction is made between partial surface joining and joining edge to edge.
The latter usually involve beaded
pouches made of ETFE sheeting. A so-
called beading, usually a flexible, PVC or
EPDM round cord, or sometimes a round
aluminium bar, is drawn in. The pieces of
sheeting are placed one on top of the
other at the welding seams and thermally
welded together. This produces a seam
about 10 mm wide, also translucent, that
is certainly thicker than the basic material,
but only visible from close to.

5

5 Walchensee power station information centre,
   Kochel am See
   Architects: Hauschild + Boesel, Munich
   Structural engineers, timber:
   Planungsgesellschaft Dittrich, Munich
   Structural engineers, membrane:
   Engineering + Design, Rosenheim
   Membrane installation: Covertex, Obing
6 Walchensee power station information centre,
   Kochel am See
   Detail of mechanical pre-tensioning, scale: 1:10
   1 ETFE membrane 0.2 mm
   2 Suction security strip ETFE membrane 0.2 mm
   3 Stainless steel edging strip clamp

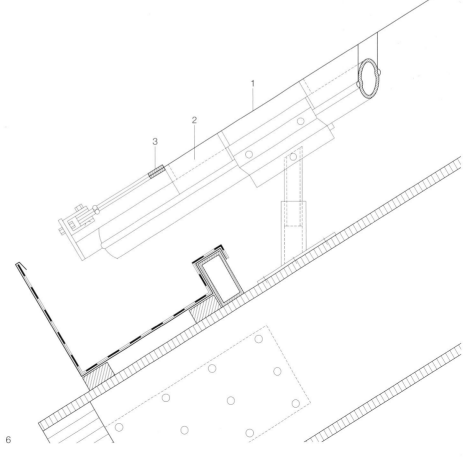

6

7 Masoala Rainforest House, Zurich Zoo
  Architects: Gautschi + Storrer, Zürich
  Structural engineers: Minikus Witta Voss, Zurich
  and a.b.t., Arnhem/NL
  Structural engineers, membrane:
  Engineering + Design, Rosenheim
  Membrane installation: Covertex, Obing
8 Earth Centre, Doncaster, UK
  Architects: Alsop & Störmer,London
  Structural engineers: Atelier One, London
  Membrane installation:
  Vector Special Projects, London

Mechanical properties

The most important mechanical property for ETFE sheeting is its stress-strain behaviour. Because of extremely high permanent strains the breaking strength of the sheeting (approx. 50 N/mm²) is less important that its behaviour up to the yield point (ill. 9).

According to the test certificates, the average mono-axially measured yield point rating at DIN EN ISO 527 is 21 N/mm² or 23 N/mm². The module measured at 21 N/mm² for NOWOFLON® (HOSTAFLON® ET 6235) is approx. 200 N/mm², and with a working load of 15 N/mm² it is approx. 550 N/mm² (ills. 9, 10).

The measurement results depend on temperature, loading rate, sample measurements, loading prehistory and the stress state. A mono-axial stress state occurs only when there is tensile stress in one direction and the sheeting is free of right-angled tension. This condition is rare in a plane load-bearing structure. In terms of fold-formation and the associated loss of dimensional stability it is even to be avoided.

In a structure, biaxial tensions with more or less marked tension differences usually occur in the two main right-angled tension directions. However, the behaviour of the sheeting differs from monoaxial behaviour (without affecting with lateral strain).

Rigidity measured at working load level is greater by a factor of approx. 1.2 than for monoaxial load in an orthotropic tension state after several loading and load relief cycles. Considerably larger factors occur when the load is first applied, which is why several loading and load relief cycles are carried out during assembly. But the rigidity calculations turn out not to imply what one might assume. Thus, raising the sheeting rigidity for a longitudinally stretched inflatable with the usual inflatable parameters by a factor of 1.2 means only a very slight increase in the calculated sheeting tension and the horizontal supporting force (approx. 3%).

Above the yield point, which is somewhat higher for biaxial than monoaxial load, the sheeting is extremely soft, so that in the fracture state deformations of up to approx. 800% occur.

The plastic range has no constructional advantages, but does mean "good-natured" material behaviour in safety terms. It does not fail suddenly, but only after a clear increase in load.

Deformations occurring in the yield region are also visible, which means very clear warning of any potential failure.

As well as this, major plastic deformations lead to larger support angles and thus to reduced horizontal support force. Another mechanical behaviour aspect is tearing strength. As a visco-elastic material, from a certain load level, sheeting creeps under continuous load. This needs to be taken into account particularly in the case of mechanically pre-stressed constructions when choosing the pre-tension level and assessing long-term load situations. Statistical appraisal of material ratings for homogeneous and isotropic EFTE sheeting suggest significantly lower variance in properties related to manufacturing than for fabric membranes, for example.

When planning the membrane roof of the centre for the Deutsche Bundestiftung Umwelt's (DBU) environmental communications centre in Osnabrück (ill. 16), a wide-ranging short- and long-term test programme was carried out into mono- and biaxial behaviour in NOWOFLON® (HOSTAFLON® ET 6235) ETFE sheeting. [1]

Other studies of ETFE sheeting are currently being carried out as part of a research project in the structural engineering department at the Technische Universität in Munich.

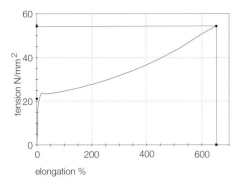

9   Stress-strain curve for NOWOFLON®
    ET 6235, thickness 200 µm, width 15 mm

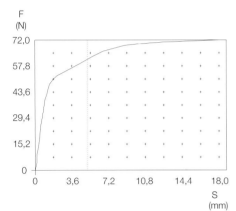

10 Force-deformation curve NOWOFLON® ET 6235,
    thickness 200 µm, width 15 mm

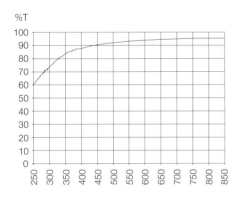

11 Overall light transmission, NOWOFLON® ET 6235
    – transparent (natural), thickness 200 µm

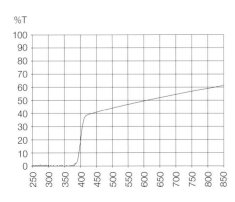

12 Overall light transmission, NOWOFLON® ET 6235
    – white, thickness 200 µm

Building physics properties

The most important criteria in terms of building physics for use as an external envelope are thermal insulation and climatic protection, sound insulation and sound absorption, as well as visual qualities.

Pneumatically supported wall or roof elements are frequently constructed with a third, taut middle layer that has no load-bearing function as a rule. In this way the enclosed air is divided between two communicating chambers with the same pressure, thus giving the system better heat insulation properties.

Because of the minimum thickness of the inflatable element at the locking lines, conventional 3-layer inflatable achieve k-values of approx. 2 W/(m²K). If the upper and lower layer of the inflatable are fastened to the primary support structure separately, the k-value can be improved by up to 20 % according to the system. (The k-value was arrived at in the calculations. It has now been superseded by the U-value).

High immission of heat energy via large transparent surfaces is applicable to the overall thermal balance of a building, but such heat gains feature mainly in the summer months.

In closed buildings, immission can be reduced by using shading systems, like for example louvres built into the inflatable. Elements that can be raised, or adequate ventilation, can also be used to get rid of the warm air. The idea of gaining available thermal energy between several layers of a transparent inflatable and storing it temporarily in ground heat storage devices, for example, is not new, but so far it has not proved economical to implement it.

The potential for fluoropolymer sheeting in the building industry in combination with other technologies is by no means exhausted. As far as the authors are aware, combining multi-layer EFTE sheeting with integrated transparent thermal insulation is still to come. As far as low sound insulation and sound absorption in sheeting systems are concerned, checks must be made each time they are used to establish what sound sources there are that could impair use. For example, if it is used for housing or offices, additional sound insulation or sound absorption layers should be planned where necessary. In cases of constant high humidity, in swimming baths or greenhouses, for example, a permanent flow of air through the inflatables can change it several times per day. This stops condensation building up in the inflatable. This can be supported by building a dryer into the fan. Condensation can also occur at the jointing points in the interior in cases of high humidity or when there is a high temperature gradient; this has to be removed through built-in channels.

The architecturally interesting optical properties of EFTE sheeting derive from the reflected, absorbed and transmitted solar component, especially in the visible light range between 390 nm and 770 nm. But transmission in the UV area (< 390 nm) can also be crucial to certain uses, e.g. hothouses, roofed lawns or swimming pools. The transmission, reflection and absorption ratio derives in each case from the material, the number of layers, the thickness of sheeting used, the angle of incidence of the light and the colour of the sheeting, arrived at by printing or tinting.

Transmission through transparent sheeting (for example NOWOFLON® and TOYOFLON®) is distributed relatively evenly over the visible radiation spectrum (ill. 11). So colours look the same under a transparent EFTE roof as they do in the open air. But by using white-tinted sheeting it is possible to block out the UV spectrum almost completely (ill. 12).

13

13 National Space Centre Museum, Leicester, UK
    Architects: Nicholas Grimshaw & Partners, London
    Structural engineers: Ove Arup & Partners, London
    Membrane installation: Skyspan, Salisbury, UK
14 Predator house Tierpark Hellabrunn, Munich
    Architect: Herbert Kochta, Munich
    Structural engineers: IPL, Ingenieurplanung und
    Leichtbau, Radolfzell (design),
    Schlaich, Bergermann und Partner, Stuttgart
    Membrane installation: Skyspan, Rimsting
15 Eden Project, St. Austell, Cornwall, UK
    Architects: Grimshaw & Partners, London
    Structural engineers: Anthony Hunt Associates,
    Cirencester
    Membrane installation: Foiltec, Bremen
16 ZUK Zentrum für Umweltkommunikation der
    Deutschen Bundesstiftung Umwelt, Osnabrück
    Architects: Herzog + Partner, Munich
    Structural engineers: Barthel und Maus, Beratende
    Ingenieure, Munich
    Membrane installation: B & O Hightex, Munich

Planning

Constructions using sheeting, like all membrane constructions, are characterized by the interplay of design and load-bearing structure, and between form, material and load. Hence architects, structural engineers and manufacturers should work together very intensively even at the design stage, especially when agreement is needed for a particular element, as thus will be granted only for the building product used (the construction type employed). One important phase in planning membrane structure is establishing form, [3] but this will not be further discussed here as there is a great deal of literature available on the subject.

Assembly

As a rule, manufacturers assemble the sheeting themselves or are present in a supervisory capacity.
Sheeting is assembled using special assembly tools which enable the pouch and its beading to be pulled into the groove of an edging element running round the structure.
Each manufacturers carries a range of their own edging elements, usually multipartite, consisting of extruded aluminium profiles. The individual parts are screwed together so that the pouch and its beading cannot slip out. This creates a so-called positive joint.
The bolt holes in the edging elements are usually so arranged that screws cannot penetrate or damage the sheeting. As an alternative to straight edging elements with restricted flexibility, it is possible to use garland cable pouches or polygonal or curved flat elements as edging devices.

Approval for use

Building products have to be approved in terms of their mechanical strength and stability, fire safety, hygiene, health and environmental suitability, safety in use, sound insulation, energy saving and thermal insulation for the particular use. Whether they can be used or not is determined by the technical specifications (standards or technical approval criteria) laid down in regional building regulations. In Germany this also includes the usual "General Building Approval and Certification" rules. According to Article 19, Paragraph 1 of the Bavarian building regulations (Bayerische Bauordnung; BayBO), a building product can be used if it does not or does not substantially deviate from the rules laid down in construction product law, in other words if it is on the Category A Building Regulation List (regulated construction products). This does not apply to ETFE sheeting. It has to be approved for use under BayBO Art. 19, Para. 3, with a "general construction regulation approval" (Art. 20), for secondary use with a "general construction regulation test certificate" (Art. 21) or in relation to a specific project with an agreement for an individual case (Art. 22).
So far ETFE sheeting has been granted only one "general construction regulation approval". This applies to the TEXLON® roof system, which consists of ETFE sheeting cushions with a constant internal pressure of 200 Pa, supported by cable bracing. Then both the NOWOFLON® and TOYOFLON® sheeting products have a "general construction regulation test certificate", but this applies only to its fire resistance properties. They are classed as flame-resistant materials under DIN 4102. So ETFE sheeting to be used for other than secondary purposes fundamentally needs agreement for an individual case from the top building authority in the state in question. But a great deal of data and experience is now available that makes it easier to asses the situation and smooth the permission-granting process.

14

15

16

17

Suggested literature:

[1] Barthel, Rainer; Burger, Norbert; Saxe, Klaus:
Eine transluzente Dachkonstruktion und Versuche
zum mechanischen Verhalten von ETFE-Folie.
In: DBZ 4/2003
[2] Franck, Adolf: Kunststoff-Kompendium.
Würzburg: Vogel Buchverlag. 2000
[3] Moritz, Karsten: Materialeinsatz und
Konfektionierung von Membranwerkstoffen.
In: Stahlbau 69, 8/2000, pp. 619–626
[4] Moritz, Karsten: Membranwerkstoffe im Hochbau.
In: Detail 6/00, pp. 1050–1058
[5] Nentwig, Joachim: Kunststoff-Folien. München:
Carl Hanser Verlag. 2000
[6] Nowofol GmbH, Siegsdorf: Produktinformationen

17 New football stadium, Munich
Architects: Herzog & de Meuron, Basel

Assessment

Regardless of "individual permission", stability and suitability for use have to be proved in every case. An ETFE sheeting construction can be broken down theoretically into a primary system (e.g. steel load-bearing system) and a secondary system (sheeting). As the primary system is usually very rigid in relation to the secondary system (exception: load-bearing cable systems) and is anyway stable in its own right, it is rare for the whole system to have to meet requirements such as deformation interaction. The adequacy of the sheeting can be established on the basis of the material specifications and realistic load ratings. As there are as yet no specific standards or guidelines for this sphere, the structural engineer has to devise the rating concept in relation to the project and agree it with the inspecting engineer. The relevant standards (e.g. DIN 1055) are used to determine loads and load overlaps. Wind loads and loads from drifting snow can be assessed more accurately by wind tunnel experiments where necessary. As a rule, the favourable effect of interacting wind loads and deformations in the soft membrane are not accounted for in wind tunnels. If roof inflatables do not slope sufficiently towards the eaves, unplanned pressure reduction or pressure failure can cause water to accumulate, and this should be considered as a special load when proving stability.

Looking ahead

The advantages ETFE sheeting offers the construction industry will lead to increased use of this plastic. One example is Herzog & de Meuron's design for the new football stadium in Munich (ill. 17), which plans a partially transparent, partially translucent envelope consisting of several thousand ETFE inflatables. This major project alone encourages a positive prognosis for the future of the material.

Metal

Diaphanous metals

Stefan Schäfer

A great selection of diaphanous metal materials is available today, ranging from perforated sheets, gratings and expanded mesh to net-like, woven and knitted fabrics. Glass is already meeting the need for highly transparent areas in buildings. What has to be addressed now is the intermediate sphere between closed and transparent envelopes. It is not only simple products used in industrial or scaffolding construction that are now being discovered by architects and used for prestigious parts of buildings like facades. Constant development of manufacturing techniques also offers new design possibilities with special material and product qualities, especially when used for building envelopes.

Diaphanous metal building envelopes

Facades have a structural aspect as well as an aspect relating to materials. Since the early days of modern architecture, the envelope has been broken down into several facade layers. This has meant that individual functions can be assigned to the individual structural layers, thus allowing for ideal use of materials. Metallic materials or semi-finished products can be easily built into an existing sequence of layers as a component, without changed the building envelope as a whole.

Perforated curtains can achieve interesting diaphanous effects depending on how far away the viewer is. From the distance, the effect is of apparently closed metal envelope, but they develop high level of transparency from other angles. Changing light and shade, sun and rain, day and night enliven the surface and make the building give a whole range of different impressions. According to the incident light, changing views are afforded into the inside of a building, and according to where you are standing you experience the surfaces as closed or much more transparent.

Perforated sheets with the finest drill holes provide high-calibre sun protection, while the view from inside is largely unimpaired. Steven Holl used perforated sheets for his pavilion in Amsterdam (ill. 9), and made the staggered overlapping of the facade layers into a concept. Grids permit right-angled viewing axes and remove diagonal viewing axes – the surface seems closed. Metal meshes create attractive semi-transparency. It is precisely by using meshes of this kind that offers those creating the building a unique chance to rethink the material quality of facade surfaces. The very idea of an "envelope" suggests lightness, permeability and a certain ability to vary appearance. Permeability is also one of the original properties of these semi-finished products, which come from industrial filtering and sieving technology. Before meshes could be discovered for the building industry, is was essential to develop a new sense of spatial boundaries. Astonishingly enough in this context, the qualities of modern building envelopes are not determined by measurable values like heat transfer coefficients or load-bearing capacity. They owe much more to more subjective criteria like transparency or material quality. For example, Dominique Perrault was using metal meshes as early as the 1980s, in the French National Library in Paris, for example, where the metal meshes seem like an internal facade offering protection against the sun.

Metal meshes, even in the technical sense, come astonishingly close to the metaphor that a building's envelope is a kind of third skin, after people's skin and clothes. Almost any kind of idea can be realized given the range of different surface structures and degrees of permeability in the material, from opaque meshes to those that are so finely woven you can hardly see them at all. This breadth is due to the fact that the manufacturing process can be individually controlled. It offers a large number of parameters for making things look different. Since the introduction of mesh-type, perforated metal facade materials for facades, buildings can be covered with a light material, like a curtain. The textile look of many meshes admits almost any possible geometry, even for very large areas. These can be executed with very comparatively little difficulty in terms of assembly and fitting. The advantages of metal facade surfaces lie in the fact that they are relatively easy to handle, need little maintenance and can be designed individually. Besides, they are mainly robust, long-lasting and reasonably cheap to manufacture. Metal facade elements suspended outside the building are also outstandingly suitable for protection against the sun.

1   "Fünf Höfe" office block, Munich
    Material: angled perforated sheet metal, tombak
    Architects: Herzog & de Meuron, Basel

General points on construction, supply and storage

Temperature-related changes of length and wind suction forces are crucial in terms of processing techniques and dimensioning. Structural measures like sliding connections, for example, and adequate joint distances for sheet metal, should be so calculated that no bending and thus undue strain on the material is possible. Extra care in fixing is needed particularly for areas with peripheral wind loads (DIN 1055, part 4). Dimensions for the individual fixing points to the support structure are arrived at by assessing the maximum individual fixing needs.

An equally important point is structural corrosion protection. If metals with different chemical properties are used, acid oxidation erosion must be inhibited: within a particular area, no rainwater can subsequently flow over baser metals, as more noble metals higher in the tension series corrode baser metals (ill. 3). An area of copper above zinc will thus always cause corrosion damage. But aluminium, lead, non-rusting and galvanized steel (traces of running rust are possible on unprotected cut edges) are safe with zinc. Mineral materials like for example cement, plaster or lime also corrode metal it moisture is also present. Here appropriate separating layers must be provided.

When metal materials are delivered or stored, measures appropriate to the material must be taken. In principle, all surface-ready metals need protection. Special transport facilities (palettes) with lifting belts are ideal here. Sheeting is often delivered "face en face", i.e. the visible surfaces are in contact and protect each other. Moisture penetration should be prevented here. In the open air it is advisable to store the palettes on a slight diagonal, so that residual water can run off. Protective film should be removed rapidly on site (remains of adhesive), and the individual manufacturer's storage instructions must be followed. Strips of metal mesh are ideally delivered rolled and covered with protective film. Local pressure loading is to be avoided at all costs: even small kinks creates irreparable visual flaws in rigid wires.

Metallic materials

Metals, in the form of chemical elements, are among the basic materials the earth is made up of. The occurrence of metal is altered locally by natural and human interventions. Transformation processes, like being washed away by rain, are inimical to local concentrations. All essential metals are subject to a natural cycle. Hence seasonal phenomena (falling leaves and annual plant growth) move about four times as much copper as human activity. Some metals are needed for human nourishment (iron, for example). Only a few heavy metal compounds, like cadmium or mercury, are polluting and seriously damaging to health.

Up to a density of < 4.5 g/cm³, metals are classified as light metals, and all the higher densities as heavy metals (table 2). Some key metals for the building industry are listed below.

Aluminium
After oxygen and silicon, aluminium is the third most common element (8.1 %) in the earth's crust. It is a silver-white, ductile light metal with good electrical conductivity; like all metals that can be used for technical purposes it does not occur naturally as an element. The processing temperatures required (over 2000 °C) and thus the cost of aluminium extraction, are very high. Aluminium is used pure or as an alloy in building. It is classified according to thickness as sheet, strip (over 0.35 mm thick), thin strip (0.21 to 0.35 mm thick) and foil (up to 0.02 mm thick).

Aluminium reflects heat extremely well. It is highly resistant to environmental effects with its naturally grey, thin, regenerative oxide skin. Because of its high resilience, it can be fixed with simple clamps and fastenings. In this way, surface perforation for point connections can be avoided.

Because of the high energy levels needed for manufacture, aluminium is seen as an expensive material, economically and ecologically. But its durable, robust, natural surface gives it a long useful life, which makes the high acquisition price entirely economical.

Lead
Bluish-grey lead is a soft-malleable, slightly toxic heavy metal. It has a silvery gleam when freshly cut but forms a thin, protective oxide layer immediately. Lead is very stable in chemically hard water; it dissolves in softened water with a high CO_2 content. Lead has very low thermal and electrical properties. It is eminently recyclable, and so the quantities extracted in recent years have declined considerably.

Lead is used in building solely as a connecting material, or as protection against radiation. The lead alloys used for these purposes are not injurious to health, chemically stable and have a limited quantitative market share (connecting sheets, drip angles etc.).

Chromium
Chromium has a silver sheen, is ductile in its pure state and is stable in contact with air, water and some acids. Chromium does not occur in its pure form in nature, but as chromium ore (chromite). Pure chromium is produced by electrolysis, and chromium-carbon alloys by reducing chromite in electrical furnaces. Chromium is used mainly as an alloy for manufacturing corrosion-resistant, heavy duty chromium and chromium-nickel steels.

Copper
Shiny red copper is a chemical heavy metal element that is relatively soft, highly ductile and after silver the best conductor of heat and electricity. The natural copper content of the earth is between approx. 3 to 290 mg/kg. In contact with the atmosphere, copper forms a natural oxide surface layer that changes materially and in terms of colour with time, and gives this material its long life.

With time, the protective layer becomes a green patina (copper carbonate). This process also depends on the geometry of the building and the composition of the air. Rain, snow, wind and certain materials in the air remove the protective layer by weathering, but it regenerates itself continuously.

The life of copper surfaces can be predetermined by assessing the removal rate. The improved air quality of the last 20 years has considerably reduced copper removal rates in relation to earlier periods. On average, European rates for copper wash-off have been determined at 0.7 to 1.5 g of copper per year per surface m². Despite its usually higher cost, using copper materials pays for itself because it lasts for so long. Copper is used in building in the form of wire, bars and fittings, and also as sheeting and tubes.

Nickel
Nickel is a silver-white, robust, very shiny heavy metal with ferro-magnetic properties. It can be forged, rolled, drawn into wire and welded. It is resistant to oxygen, water and non-oxidizing acids, so it can also be used for tempering surfaces. Nickel occurs naturally in compound form, frequently accompanied by iron ores. Nickel is a popular alloy metal for stainless steel, various nickel alloys, for manufacturing NiCd accumulators, and as a catalyst. It is used in small quantities as a pure metal in the chemical industry.

Steel
Steel differs from iron in having a smaller proportion of undesirable impurities that define its properties (including carbon, phosphorous, sulphur. Steel is scarcely

2: Metal property profiles

Material	titanium	steel	iron	RSH-steels	nickel	aluminium	copper	zinc	tin	lead
Chemical symbol	Ti		Fe		Ni	Al	Cu	Zn	Sn	Pb
Density [g/cm³] at 25°C	4.51	7.8	7.87	7.9	8.9	2.7	8.96	7.13	7.29	11.34
Elasticity module [GPa]	110	210	211.4	195	200	65	70	69.4/104.5	45.8/16.1	58.2/49.9
Thermal expansion coefficient [10⁻⁶/°C]	9	11.7	12.1	17.3	11.4–14	21–24	16.2–20	31	29	23.5
Thermal conductivity [W/(m K)]	22	65	80.4	14	15 [90.9]	160	150	116	35.3	66.8
Melting point [°C]	1,668	1,510	1,538		1,455	660.32	1,084	419.5	231.9	327
Boiling point [°C]	3,287	3,000	2,861		2,913	2,519	2,562	907	2,602	1,749
Occurrence [mg/kg]/[%]	0.6		4.7		0.008	8.1	0.007	0.012	0.00022	0.0014
Price approx. [€ je ton]	40 – 50,000	2,600 – 3,000 (carbon steel)	150		7,100	1,450	1,540	870	4,400	500

ever used in its pure form, without surface protection.

A distinction is made between fine (0.35 to 3 mm thick), medium (3 to 4.75 mm thick) and thick sheet steel (over 4.74 mm thick). The sheet steel described in this chapter is in the fine category. As a rule, steel strips up to 1 m wide are processed by the coils, at material thicknesses up to 0.75 mm. Steel panels are made as standard in dimensions up to approx. 2× 4 m.

The low alloy construction steel field includes steels that quickly rust on the surface, but do not rust any further after a time (e.g. CORTEN®). The corroded surface forms a weather-proof protective layer for the steel underneath (ill. 8). But as this process is continuous in permanently wet conditions, "rusted" facades like these must be able to dry out completely from time to time. It must be borne in mind that the washed-off corrosion can produce striation and rust trails in adjacent areas.

Steel is generally a reasonably priced, very durable material with no ecological disadvantages.

Stainless steel

Stainless steel is a high-quality, rust-free steel created as an alloy with chromium (min. 10.5 %) or manganese. Over 120 kinds have been developed to date. Stainless steel is generally categorized as non-rusting because of a regenerative, insoluble passive layer, but problems with corrosion do still occur. Stainless steel can corrode in critical surroundings, e.g. in air containing salt, rain containing chlorine or in condensed water.

Higher proportions of individual alloy elements like chromium, nickel, molybdenum, manganese or copper improve corrosion resistance but also frequently change the steel's properties. Because of its increased chromium-nickel content,

stainless steel is expensive and usually available only in the form of thin sheets, technical joints and fastenings or small elements.

Alongside the usual collective term stainless steel, terms like V2A, V4A or INOX are also found. Non-rusting stainless steels are usually more precisely known by the allotted material number, and where appropriate the short name, which contains information about chemical composition.

Stainless steel is considerably more expensive than ordinary steel, but does not need additional corrosion protection and is thus extremely durable.

Titanium

Titanium is silvery-white and ductile. It is the tenth most common element in the earth's crust, with a share of 0.6 %. Since the introduction of a reliable titanium extraction process in the 50s, two categories of basic titanium material have been developed:

pure titanium, consisting of 99.2 % titanium, plus oxygen, carbon and iron, and titanium alloys with 80–98 % titanium plus aluminium, vanadium, tin, chromium and others. For different kinds of pure titanium have a strength range of 290 to 740 N/mm^2, subject to differing oxygen content;

titanium alloys have strength over 1200 N/mm^2, allied with good toughness. Titanium alloys with palladium and nickel-molybdenum are considerably more resistant to corrosion.

Titanium's good corrosion resistance, high level of toughness with a low own weight and outstanding mechanical and thermal capacity are important reasons for its wide range of uses, in air and space travel, for example. Titanium is 42 % lighter than steel, with the same toughness, but much more expensive.

3: Metal stress series against hydrogen

Metal		normal potential V
Gold	Au	+ 1.50
Mercury	Hg	+ 0.85
Silver	Ag	+ 0.80
Copper	Cu	+ 0.35
Hydrogen	H	0
Lead	Pb	− 0.12
Tin	Sn	− 0.14
Nickel	Ni	− 0.23
Cadmium	Cd	− 0.40
Iron	Fe	− 0.44
Chromium	Cr	− 0.56
Zinc	Zn	− 0.76
Manganese	Mn	− 1.05
Aluminium	Al	− 1.68
Magnesium	Mg	− 2.34
Potassium	K	− 2.92

2 Metal property profiles
3 Metal stress series against hydrogen
4 "Sejima Building", Gifu, Japan
  Material: wire mesh elements
  Architects: Kazuyo Sejima and Ruye Nishizawa, Tokyo
5 "Münchner Tor" office building
  Material: perforated sheet metal
  Architects: Allmann Sattler Wappner, Munich
6 Advertising agency in Hamburg
  Material: perforated sheet metal, polyspectrally anodized
  Architect: Carsten Roth, Hamburg

7

Zinc

Bluish-white zinc is a brittle metal that is very shiny on its cut surfaces; it can be rolled at approx. 120 °C. It is usually used in low alloy form (with small proportions of copper and/or titanium).

Because it forms a protective layer naturally, zinc does not need additional corrosion protection. It is used above all to prevent surface corrosion in other metals. Zinc's mechanical and technological qualities are dramatically increased in alloys with titanium. Scrap zinc is practically 100 % recyclable. If zinc surfaces are wet over long periods with chemically aggressive water ("acid rain") they can be attacked to a measurable extent, i.e. the water that runs off contains zinc ions in solution. As zinc is non-toxic, unlike many heavy metals, rainwater of this kind is harmless.

Zinc sheeting can be handled very easily even at low temperatures, and also in long lengths (up to 6 m and more) because of good thermal expansion characteristics. The sheets used are 0.7 to 1.5 mm thick and up to 1000 mm wide. Panels are processed in sizes up to approx. 1000 × 3000 mm. Prefabricated roof sheeting is approx. 0.7 mm thick. Zinc is now one of the cheapest "anti-corrosion metals", and is also used very widely because of its durability and health safety.

Tin

Tin is a shiny, silver-white and relative soft heavy metal, known in three forms: grey, cubically aligned alpha-tin tends to pulverize gradually at low temperatures (tin plague in organ-pipes). Above 13.25 °C alpha-tin shifts to the more common, white, tetragonally aligned beta-tin. This is easily written on and can be rolled out into a wafer-thin film (tinfoil). Above 162 °C tin becomes brittle, the rhombically aligned gamma-tin, which rubs down to a grey powder. Pure tin has a relatively low melting point: it can be melted in a candle-flame. At room temperature, tin is stable with air and water, as it gradually becomes covered with a thin, anti-corrosive oxide layer. Over a third of the tin used today derives from recycling. Almost half the tin produced is used for tinning metals, giving them an extremely durable, silvery sheen.

Alloys

Metallic mixtures of at least two elemental metals are known as alloys, regardless of their components. They can have completely different properties from their starter elements. Alloys are widespread in building, where elemental metals are quite rare. Modern materials can contain over a dozen different metal alloys – and there is still no end to the possibilities. Thus the materials on the market fluctuate considerably, and new variants are constantly added.

One particularly promising development is nitrogen alloy steel, as this can combine great hardness with very good ductility; light metal alloys combine a low own weight with great hardness, and are not sensitive to corrosion. The more recent aluminium alloys contain the very light lithium and are highly scratch-resistant - they are frequently used in the aerospace industry. Copper alloys have been known for centuries – copper and tin make bronze. Materials for mechanically very highly loaded bearings are made of copper and lead. The so-called superalloy group retain great strength even at high temperatures as a result of tailored surface treatment. They are used for turbine blades among other things. Metals with high melting points, tungsten for example, are always used when high working temperatures occur, in space travel, for example.

The actual manufacturing processes are also in a constant state of development. The best-known of the many possible alloys are:

· brass (55 to 90 % copper, 45 to 10 % zinc)
· tombac (ill.1)(brass with a high copper content)
· tin bronze (phosphorous bronze)
· titanium zinc
· monel (67 % nickel, up to 33 % copper etc.)

7 Summerhouse in Dyngby, Denmark
   Material: expanded metal tiles, pre-oxydized
   Architect: Claus Hermansen, Viby
8 House in Amsterdam
   Material: sheet Corten steel, round perforation
   Architects: Heren 5 architecten, Amsterdam

Surfaces

Some lasting anti-corrosion measures are usually taken, as well as addressing the visual qualities of a surface. This particularly affects steel-based, corrosion-sensitive materials.

Woven and knitted fabrics are a special case among the diaphanous building materials discussed here, as they are based on wire. Because of their porosity and surface structure, it is very difficult to treat or finish woven materials after the weaving process. Hence the wire strands are usually surface-finished. As there is high mechanical stress in the loom, the only suitable surfaces are those not sensitive to scratching.

There are three anti-corrosion devices:

• naturally protected surfaces
• metallic coating
• non-metallic coating

Naturally protected surfaces

Naturally protected surfaces (such as aluminium, stainless steel, zinc, tin, copper, titanium) do not need additional protection in normal weather conditions (ill. 9). They have self-forming, regenerative passive layers. These layers are sometimes made artificially passive by various processes. This is faster and more precise, as the layer thicknesses achieved form evenly.

Aluminium can be anodized in an anodic oxidation process, producing a variety of shades, usually yellowish. Hot, alkaline salt solutions are used to make steel surfaces corrosion-resistant by covering them with a thin, brown-to-black film of iron oxide. Iron is phosphate-coated chemically, aluminium is treated in electro-chemical baths, and carbon steel is rendered passive with alkaline additions. Metals with naturally protected surfaces are ideally suited to weaving.

Metallic coatings

Metallic coatings are applied to strips, panels or wire either galvanically, by electrochemical separation from liquid solutions, vapour-deposited in a gaseous state or plated in solid form. Aqueous, acid or alkaline solutions are used as electrolytes when galvanizing. The anodes are usually made of the metal to be separated.

For example, brass is coppered using a copper sulphate ($CuSO_4$) solution. Processes intended to apply very thin layers (e.g. vacuum processes) are becoming increasingly important.,

Enamelling and galvanizing are two of the most tried-and-tested processes. Enamel is a glassy covering with materials including silicon oxide, which is applied by immersion, spraying or dusting and then baked on at approx. 800 °C. Enamel powder can be used in thicknesses between 80 and 200 µ. This makes the surface proof against acids and alkalis, able to provide electrical insulation and impact, shock and bend resistant.

In galvanizing, a zinc coating approx. 0.1 mm thick is applied to the pre-treated steel parts in a liquid zinc immersion bath. The zinc bath is at a temperature of 450 °C, and the immersion lasts a few minutes.

To raise resistance to corrosion, the zinc coatings are also chromed, oiled or covered with plastic (e.g. duplex process). The original metal is no longer visible and because of the thin protective coating is sensitive to mechanical stress, especially around open edges, perforation and welding seams. Freshly galvanized surfaces have to be further treated or alternatively exposed to some months of weathering before they can take an additional coating of colour.

Metal-coated wire is usually well suited to weaving.

Non-metallic coatings

Non-metallic coatings include transparent or opaque varnishes and also differing thicknesses of calendered fiilm (strip coating). Polyester is usually used for this. The idea behind electrostatic powder coating is based on the fact that parts with opposite electrical charges attract each other. Hence all thermally stable solids are suitable for powder coating, in which electrostatically charged coating powered is sprayed evenly on to the earthed item and then solidified in a melting and hardening process at 160 to 200 °C. When using plastic powder, the layer thicknesses in this finishing process are between 30 and 500 µ. Low-bake paints are paints whose molecules combine through chemical reactions between polyester and melamine resin when heated to 80 to 350 °C. Low-bake paints produce shiny, mechanically durable and corrosion-proof films. Hence they are very important in industrial metal painting, e.g. for car bodies or household appliances. One key advantage of post-coating lies in building physics. It is possible to build up anti-drum coatings (sound insulation) and vibration-inhibiting coatings. Industrially applied robust paint is also increasingly used to permit difficult shaping processes during subsequent work (table 10).

As well as the other pre-intermediate and post-treatments mentioned in this report, there are also mechanical processes that bring about visual as well as functional changes. In stucco patterning, for example, the stability of the sheet metal itself can be clearly increased by the embossed micro-structures.

For cleaning, finishing and fixing (shot peening) the metal parts are usually sprayed with stainless steel balls, glass beads, clean corundum or ceramic beads.

Difficult and bulky parts that cannot be polished mechanically are polished electrically to smooth them or to clean welding seams.

In brushing, ornamental micro-fine structures are polished into the surface of the material by roller or with rotating brushes, thus creating a light-dependent glossy structure.

Non-metallic coatings are less suitable for protecting woven metal against corrosion, as the surfaces are less loadable and not as scratch-resistant.

9

10: Organic coatings for metal surfaces

Coating material	abbreviation	layer thickness μm	corrosion protection class according to DIN 55928-8
Paint systems			
Polyester	SP	10	II
Polyester	SP	25	III
Polyurethane	PUR	25	III
High-durable polymers	HDP	25	III
Polyvinylidene fluoride	PVDF	25	III
Polyvinyl chloride-Plastisol	PVC (P)	100 – 200	III
Sheeting systems			
Polyvinyl chloride	PVC (F)	100 – 200	III
Polyvinyl chloride	PVF (F)	40	III

9   Pavilion in Amsterdam
    Material: sheet metal, perforated, with patina
    Architects: Steven Holl Architects, New York
10 Organic coatings for metal surfaces

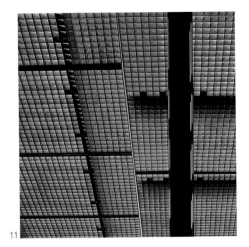

11

Diaphanous semi-finished sheet products
In order to make clearer distinctions, this section looks at semi-finished products made by further processing – milling, punching, cutting, drilling, stamping etc. – mainly from sheet metal between 0.008 mm and 3 mm thick.

General construction notes
Thin-walled and diaphanous metals usually offer very poor or no insulation. Hence they are often used in multi-shell structures in which only the outer skin is made of metal.
As a rule, the needs of building physics are met in the layers behind. Thus the stresses to the outermost shell are limited to mechanical weather protection, protection against corrosion and various mechanical strains (from wind, for example).
Associated with this is something of a contradiction: an envelope that is fully effective in terms of building physics has to exist already before parts of this layer can be re-covered with perforated materials in front.
Single-shell structures can be used inside the building.

Stabilizing and joining
Metal surfaces usually have membranous cross-sections and are thus primarily unstable.
For large-size sheets in particular, therefore, adequate statical reinforcement has to be provided, by introducing flanged edges, for example.
The flanges are also used for fixing the sheets to the supporting structure. This often determines the pattern of joints on the surface of the building. Other possible means of reinforcement are stiffening brackets fixed at the back, flat folded areas or composite sheets with sufficient rigidity in their own right.
New solutions for stabilizing unstable metal areas are moving towards developing glass laminates with intermediate layers of metal.
Technically speaking, it is possible to distinguish between non-penetrating (invisible) and penetrating (visible) fixing. All kinds of fixing have to be reversible to facilitate subsequent maintenance and repair.
Unpleasant noises can be produced by thermal expansion at points where metal components are in contact. This is avoided by fitting plastic spacers underneath at the points of contact.
The number of connection points needed depends on vertical load dispersion and

the prevailing wind suction forces. A large number of other jointing techniques are available when statical issues are not so important. Flat surfaces with open, flush joints are very popular. Then there are flush-butted closed surfaces, overlapping scaley surfaces or surfaces with connecting elements. In terms of jointing, point (screws, rivets, brackets) or linear (soft and hard soldering, gluing, clamping, welding), connection techniques are used according to the metal. Only clamped or suspended solutions are ideal.

Summary of semi-finished products
The products described below do not have a closed surface and are porous to a certain extent. In suitable forms, they produced the translucent light effects described above. Quite often individual parameters (percentage of openness, minimum aperture diameters, pattern forming, material etc.) are crucially important, so that the products are frequently custom made.

11 Refectory and mess at the Army Officers' School in Dresden, sunshading canopy
Material: gratings
Architects: Auer + Weber + Partner, Stuttgart
12 Balcony parapet, Munich
Material: laser-cut sheet steel, painted
Architects: Hild und K., Munich

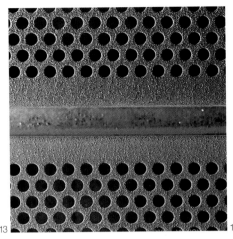

13 14 15

Perforated sheets

Modern broad and strip presses and CNC (Computerized Numerical Control) punching machines make it possible to punch holes from 1 mm to approx. 500 mm from sheet metal. In industrial processes, either individual sheets are used, or strips direct from the coil (roll strip).

The difference between the punching and milling processes lies in the tools used, and the feed direction and speed needed.

While the punching movement is mono-axial and at right angles to the sheet, modern CNC machines can handle all three movement axes. Almost every hole diameter that is technically possible can be achieved with individual hole gauges. The rule is that the size of the hole should not be greater than the thickness of the metal. The fundamental distinctions are:

- round perforation, straight or staggered
- square perforation
- slot perforation, running longitudinally or diagonally
- rhomboid and decorative perforation

In so-called pull-through perforation, differently rounded edges are created on each side. According to the press used, a whole variety of punching combinations are possible, including customized patterns.

All the punching processes have the effect of corrugating the sheet metal because of the perforation energy, and it has to be straightened after punching. It is then cut to size, and the edges treated if necessary. Special versions are also possible: punched perforated sheets can also be shaped into corrugated or trapezoid form (ills. 19, 20, 21).

Particular attention has to be paid to controlling the distance between holes at the edge of the sheets. Holes that have been cut into or edged should be avoided at all costs.

Planned, formally satisfying edges can be created with varying distances between holes along the edges of the hole fields. The light steel material should be between 0.5 and about 6 mm thick. Larger versions over 6 m thick are possible only with softer materials. The following dimensions can be supplied:

- small format (1,000 × 2,000 mm)
- medium format (1,250 × 2,500 mm)
- large format (1,500 × 3,000 m)

- super format (1,600 × 4,000 mm)
- coils up to 1,250 mm wide and a maximum 2 mm thick

Individual cuts and panel dimensions can be prepared to order.

Perforated sheets are in common use in the building industry. The wide range of possible uses apart from exhibitions and interior design included facade cladding, sunshading louvres, and infills for parapets and balconies.

Comparatively simple handling (like thin sheeting), the high degree of industrial prefabrication and the wide range of finishes available make for a reasonably priced construction product. Another economic advantage of perforated sheeting is the wide range of possible uses in lightweight construction, as large savings in material can be made because of the proportion of holes.

The continuous development of CNC production machines has now meant that a high degree of precision is possible even for customized sheeting. The three-dimensional feed geometry of CNC milling machines means that the milling pattern is no longer dependent on the shape

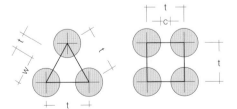

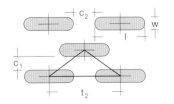

16

13 round perforation, Corten steel
14 square perforation, stainless steel
15 triangular perforation, stainless steel
16 diagrammatic symbols for dimensioning perforation types, examples:
round perforation in staggered rows (top left)
round perforation in straight rows (top right)
slot perforation in staggered rows (below)

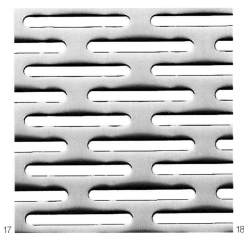

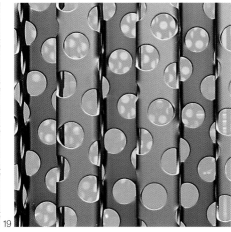

17

18

19

of the hole (ill. 12). Almost any shape can be cut, though attention must be paid to the residual stability of the remaining sheet material. A particularly interesting possibility seem to be the direct transfer of vector-based data from CAD applications, which almost every architectural practice has available nowadays. Surface engraving is also possible because the tool head can be positioned in different ways.

But the secret of successful milling is correct matching of the mechanical parameters: tool diameter, rotation and feed speed, and also material behaviour. Establishing these fundamental technical connections and conditions needs a certain amount of experience, especially for customized orders, and usually a few trial runs.

DIN abbreviations for perforations:

a_0	relative free perforation
a_1	first external sheet dimension
a_2	measure for perforated area parallel to sheet measure a_1
b_1	second external sheet dimension
b_2	measure for perforated area parallel to sheet measure b_1
c	web width
c_1	side web (slot perforation)
c_2	head web (slot perforation)
e_1, e_2	width of edging strip parallel to measure a_1
f_1, f_2	width of edging strip parallel to measure b_1
F	perforated sheet size in m² (without edge)
G_L	perforated sheet weight in kg (without edge)
k	blade clearance
l	hole length
L	slot perforation
$L_g; L_{ge}$	slot perforation in straight lines (e = slot perforation angular)
$L_v; L_{ve}$	slot perforation in staggered rows (e = slot perforation angular)

$L_{gv}; Lg_{ve}$	slot perforation in staggered rows (e= slot perforation angular)
N	number of holes by area F, N = n · F applies
n	number of holes per m²
Q	square perforation
Q_g	square perforation in straight rows
Q_v	square perforation in staggered rows
Q_d	square perforation in diagonally staggered rows
R	round perforation
R_g	round perforation in straight rows
R_v	round perforation in staggered rows
R_d	round perforation in diagonally staggered rows
s	sheet thickness
t	hole division
t_1	cross division (slot perforation)
t_2	longitudinal perforation (slot perforation)
w	hole width
we	corner measurement with square hole we = 1,414 · w

17 slot perforation, stainless steel
18 pull-through perforation, stainless steel
19 round perforation, angled perforated sheet, tombak
20 sheet metal profiles
E = flat
L = striped
N = grooved
M = micro-profiling
T = trapezoid profiling
W = corrugated profiling
21 profiling corrugated sheet metal
a corrugation profile
h = corrugation height (typically: 6 to 50 mm)
b_1 - corrugation length (typically: 15 to 200 mm)
b trapezoidal profile
h = corrugation height (typically: 10 to 100 mm)
b_1 = corrugation length (typically: 30 to 150 mm)
b_3 and b_4 usually to order

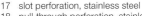

E

L

N

M

T

W

20

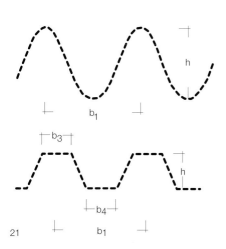

21

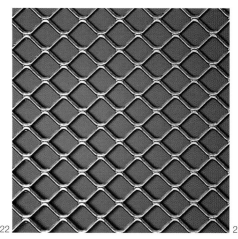

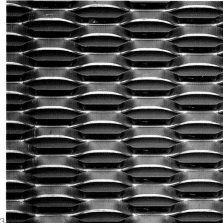

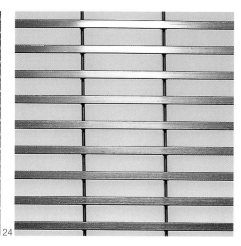

22   23   24

Expanded meshes

Expanded metals or expanded gratings are semi-finished products with shallow, diamond-shaped openings usually produced in panels or strips by means of offset cut lengths.

There is no loss of material through waste: the apertures simply emerge in the cutting process. The material between the cuts still holds together, and does not have to be subsequently woven or welded.

Expanded mesh can be cut to size as wished, without losing its stability. Possible mesh shapes are diamonds, squares, round holes, or special meshes in panels or cut to size.

Materials used other than iron and steel are as a rule aluminium or light metal alloys, and also copper, brass, nickel, bronze and zinc.

Light expanded meshes are often used to carry rendering (previously simple wire mesh).

Their high stability and comparatively low weight also makes them extremely stable in large areas as facade elements.

Expanded mesh is ideal as a "curtain" for large, air-permeable facade openings, like multi-storey car-park facades, for example.

Other possible uses are to cover ventilator openings, filtering, false ceilings, sightscreens etc. The follow terms apply to expanded mesh:

- A mesh unit is formed by the metal webs surrounding an aperture
- The mesh length is the distance from one node – seen along the long diagonal of the trapezium – to the next
- The web width is the widths of the material remaining between the apertures.
- The web thickness is the thickness of the material used
- The node length is the distance between two adjacent long diagonals of the openings
- The node width is about twice the web width

Gratings

Gratings are often made of steel, stainless steel or aluminium, and from other materials on request. They comprise slotted bearer and filler bars that are pressed together (pressed gratings) and/or electrically welded (welded gratings). The right-angled meshes created in this way are available in a variety of mesh sizes. The

dimensions of the opposite end meshes are equal. The edges of the individual grids are set in a profiled metal strip of flat material or beading strip, and thus stabilized. Individual gratings intended to be walked on should not be square, to avoid confusion about the direction of the load-bearing bar when fitting. Different surfaces (e.g. anti-slip) are achieved with profiled bar edges.

Gratings can also be used as facade grids. They are available in every possible height and thickness. However, 1400 mm should not be exceeded for diagonal bar directions. In theory any bearer bar length can be manufactured, but statical requirements impose limits.

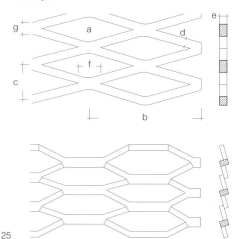

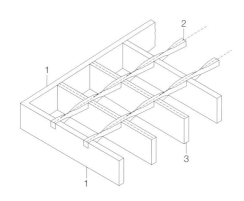

22   expanded metal, aluminium
23   expanded metal, aluminium
24   gratin, stainless steel
25   two different examples of expanded metal
     a mesh, b mesh length,
     c mesh width, d web width, e web thickness
     f node length g node width
26   welded pressed grating scheme
     1 edge bar 2 transverse bar 3 support bar
27   ways of weaving metal fabrics
     a basket-weave, b ribbed weave,
     c twilled, d twilled ribbed,
     e ribbed armoured, f long mesh,
     g five-strand twilled, h multiplex

25   26

Metal fabrics

Metal fabrics consist of round or flat wires, strands or cables. The metals used include untreated iron, galvanized steel, stainless steel and chromium-nickel steel, as well as aluminium, bronze, copper, brass, titanium and tin, where required. As with woven textiles, the longitudinal wires (warp) can be woven in a variety of forms with the lateral wires (weft). Metal fabrics are produced on special weaving looms. The most important weave forms are described below.

Basket or calico weave

This is the most common form of weave used for metal fabrics (ill. 1a). It allows great precision and the most even spacings. To achieve a better positioning of the warp and weft, a strong curvature of the wires is necessary at the points of contact. This, in turn, results in a rough surface texture. The greater the ratio between the width of the meshes (w) and the diameter of the wire (d), the more subject to displacement the mesh will be. A ratio of less than 3:1 (w:d) is, therefore, recommended.

Ribbed or corduroy weave

A special form of basket weave is where the warp wires are considerably thicker than the weft wires (ill. 1b).
The tight alignment of adjoining weft wires results in what is known as a "zero mesh". The almost triangular form of the openings created with this kind of weave are visible when viewed from the side and result in a homogeneous architectural appearance. By subjecting the finished mesh to a subsequent rolling process (calendering), the surface roughness can be reduced. The mesh can be easily bent to shape about the axis of the thick warp wires.

Twilled weave

Twilled weave (ill. 27c) results in less stressing of the wires during the weaving process.
The geometry of the weave means that the radii of curvature of the wires are only half as great as those in basket weaves, so that the strains at the crankings are much smaller. Fine-mesh fabrics are manufactured almost exclusively in this type of weave, which allows the use of relatively large wire gauges. With increasing cohesion (the number of wires crossed in one weave), the precision of the mesh decreases, but the surface smoothness increases.

Twilled ribbed weave

Closely aligned weft wires are woven in a twilled type of weave (ill. 27d) and pressed together. There is always a weft wire over and under every warp wire. Where the wire diameters are the same, twice as many weft wires are used as in normal ribbed weaving. The outcome is a very dense, mechanically resilient weave with an extremely smooth, stable surface and fine, pore-like openings.

Ribbed armoured weave

This type of weave (ill. 27e) is a reversed form of ribbed weave.
The closely aligned warp wires have a much smaller diameter than the strong weft wires. The very precise mesh formed with this type of weave is distinguished by fine openings oblique to the surface plane. The fabric itself has a remarkably high mechanical strength and can be readily shaped about the axis of the thicker wires.

Long-mesh weave

With a mesh ratio of 1:3, this type of weave (ill. 27f) has great cohesion. If the direction of the weave is reversed, The correct term is broad-mesh weave. To achieve greater stability, wires of different thicknesses may be used for warp and weft.

Five-strand twilled weave

In this type of mesh, groups of five parallel wires are woven together in both directions to produce a very smooth, easily cleaned surface (ill. 27g) with a regular chequer pattern.

Multiplex mesh

Multiplex mesh is a special form of weave, consisting of a four-strand arrangement (ill. 27h). Strands of single wires are laid out parallel to each other in both directions to form a large number of tiny, pore-like openings.

Special mention should also be made of types of mesh in which rigid metal wires are combined with woven, very soft metal strands. The wires are set out parallel to each other in their own plane, while the softer strands assume a zigzag form as a result of the weaving process. These meshes are very easily rolled up. With an individual wire diameter of over 3 mm the wires require a twisted wave geometry, and are rolled without pre-tension.
With classical types of weave, continuous strips can be obtained up to eight metres in width. This means a clear reduction of

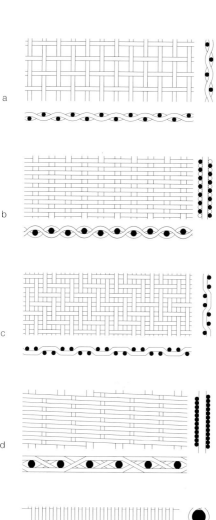

a

b

c

d

e

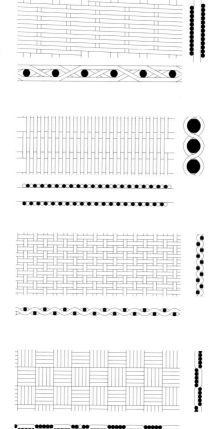

f

g

h

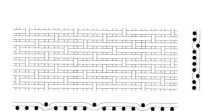

27

28

29

30

awkward seams and connecting elements because of the relatively high weave stability.

Metal fabrics are available untreated, painted, anodized or pickled (passivated). As well as this, other individual surface finishes are available on request. The wires are subject to tight constraints in terms of dimensional (diameter) tolerances, yield point and surface quality.

Metal fabric quality

As a means of determining the quality of metal fabrics in Germany, the following criteria are defined (in German industrial standard DIN 4189):

- Mesh width (w) or (mw)
  The clear space between adjoining wires is defined for both the warp and weft directions.

- Wire diameter (d)
  The wire diameter is defined prior to weaving.
  Slight changes in diameter can occur during the manufacturing process.

- Fineness of mesh
  This is defined in terms of the number of meshes per inch measured between wire axes.
  Care should be taken in this context, since there may be certain differences between unit measurements, depending on the various trade sources.
  The fineness of mesh is specified as a number. For different degrees of fineness, different unit dimensions may be used (6.16 mm; French inch 27.07 mm; British inch 25.4 mm).

- Open (sieve) area (Ao or Fo)
  The area of mesh spacings is given as a percentage of the entire mesh area.

- Number of stitches (per cm²)
  The number of stitches is given per square centimetre.

- Fabric thickness (D)
  The thickness of the fabric will depend on the wire diameter.

Fabric properties

There are six quality levels in all, which are denoted with numbers from 0 to 5. At the upper end of the quality scale, resistance to the displacement of wires is greater.

Through a combination of the criteria defining fabric quality (as described above), it is possible to determine the properties of the individual fabric types in advance.

Technically speaking, metal mesh materials are extremely efficient and versatile. In addition to their industrial uses as filters, sieves, process strips and in the field of sound absorption, they now have a wide range of applications in architecture. This applies especially to facade construction, wall and soffit linings, and in forming partitions, falling guards and interior décor. There is even scope for the use of fine-mesh stainless-steel products as floor finishes – as matting that requires no preliminary subfloor measures.

Because it is so easily rolled, metal fabric is outstandingly suitable for mobile sun-, wind- or sight-screening. The required shade criteria can also be met with the fabric thicknesses available.

The material is extremely easy to maintain and clean. Even areas exposed to weathering are virtually maintenance free, have unlimited durability and are completely recyclable.

From certain thicknesses, metal fabrics are no longer separable – i.e. they cannot be cut to shape – and are then custom-produced. They can be supplied as rolls, strips or punched out sections. In addition to the production of small, medium and large batches, many firms are prepared to manufacture individual elements to order. Like textiles, metal fabrics can also be installed in a pre-stressed state. Structural advantages derive from high loadability (e.g. in terms of wind) combined with low weight per unit area. Use in plane load-bearing structures can also be considered; this raises questions of surface form.

Special details – clamps, brackets etc. – have to be devised for load transfer at points of attachment to avoid separation of the metal wires.

Details from the textile industry can only be applied to a limited extent because metal fabrics are less flexible.

Metal grilles and knitted fabrics
Wire-fabric or mesh products are complemented by a range of related materials, including flat layers of wire or strips (e.g. metal gratings). Stable spot-welded or pressed grilles are made from the crossed, orthogonal layers of wire. They are produced in different mesh sizes and material thicknesses, and from materials like galvanized or ungalvanized steel, aluminium and stainless steel. The widely used corrugated grille is actually a coarse-mesh fabric with canvas binding and spirals of bars, pre-offset in both directions. All the grilles can usually be made to measure, and are available as standard sheeting.

They are frequently used in industrial construction; common reinforcement mats may also be included in this category. Thanks to simple industrialized mass production, products of this kind are very reasonable in price.

Net materials are a special case in this context. Typologically, they are single-layer mesh products, consisting of parallel steel cables joined together at offset nodes. Nets of this kind possess great three-dimensional flexibility and mesh stability and are of minimal weight. As a result, they are especially suitable for wide-span open structures such as aviaries. They are also stretched over large areas of rocky slopes in mountainous regions to protect against falling rocks and avalanches. In building, nets are sometimes also combined with other materials, e.g. as transparent "armour" for dry natural stone walls.

Knitted metal fabrics resemble conventional knitted products in that they consist of a virtually endless thread wound in a series of stitches row by row to create an additive area. Knitted metal fabrics have been applied hitherto mainly as internal finishings and in filter technology. They can also be used for sunshading – in the cavity between panes of double glazing, for example.

31

28 Bertelsmann pavilion EXPO 2000
    Material: stainless steel fabric
    Architects: Becker, Gewers, Kühn + Kühn, Berlin
29 Expomedia Light Cube, Saarbrücken
    Material: stainless steel fabric
    Architects: Kramm & Strigl, Darmstadt
30 Aviary in Tierpark Hellabrunn, Munich
    Material: steel wire netting, cantilevered
    Architects: Jörg Gribl, Munich
    Consultant: Frei Otto, Stuttgart
    Structural Engineering: Büro Happold, Berlin
31 Herz-Jesu-Kirche, Munich
    wall hanging
    Material: metal fabric, tombak
    Architects: Allmann Sattler Wappner, Munich
    Artists: Lutzenberger + Lutzenberger,
    Bad Wörishofen

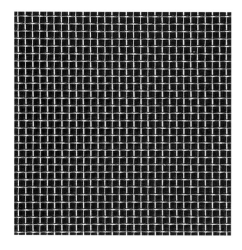

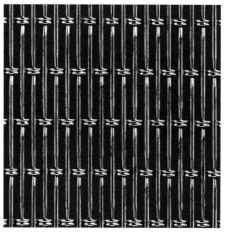

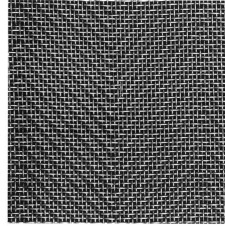

Material:	stainless steel
Weave type	basket weave
Transparency:	65 %
Wire thickness:	warp wire 1 mm
	weft wire 1 mm
Usual width:	1 m
Weight: approx.	2.7 kg/m²
Mesh width:	4 mm
Manufacturer:	Carl Beisser GmbH
Product:	stainless steel fabric

Material:	stainless steel
Weave type:	long mesh with double wires (twin)
Transparency:	approx. 50 %
Wire thickness:	dependent on use
Usual width:	up to 2.50 m
Weight:	according to specification
Manufacturer:	Haver & Boecker
Product:	stainless steel fabric, "Egla"

Material:	copper
Weave type:	twilled
Transparency:	29 %
Wire thickness:	warp wire 1 mm
	weft wire 1 mm
Usual width:	1 m
Weight:	approx. 6 kg/m²
Mesh width:	1.18 mm
Manufacturer:	Carl Beisser GmbH
Product:	copper wire fabric

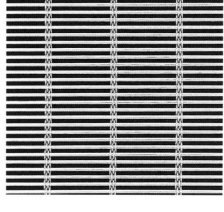

Material:	stainless steel
Weave type:	basket weave with braids (warp) and rods (weft)
Transparency:	43 %
Wire thickness:	warp cable 2.5 mm
	weft bar 2 mm
Usual width:	6–8 m
Weight:	approx. 7.8 kg/m²
Manufacturer:	Gebr. Kufferath AG
Product:	stainless steel fabric, "Baltic"

Material:	stainless steel
Weave type:	basket weave with braids (warp) and rods (weft)
Transparency:	44 %
Wire thickness:	warp cable group 4 × 1 mm
	weft bar 2 mm
Usual width:	6–8 m
Weight:	approx. 6.8 kg/m²
Manufacturer:	Gebr. Kufferath AG
Product:	stainless steel fabric, "Lago"

Material:	stainless steel
Weave type:	special: spiral weave
Transparency:	50 %
Wire thickness:	flat strip twisted to spiral 7 × 1 mm round rods 7 mm
Usual width:	on demand
Weight:	approx. 8.9 kg/m²
Manufacturer:	Gebr. Kufferath AG
Product:	stainless steel fabric. "Escale"

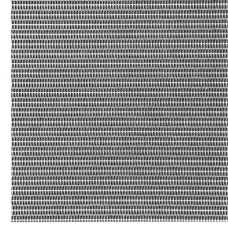

Material:	stainless steel
Weave type:	basket weave
Transparency:	30 %
Wire thickness:	warp wire 0.035 mm
	weft bar 0.035 mm
Usual width:	up to 1.5 m
Weight:	approx. 0.209 kg/m²
Mesh width:	0.04 mm, filter fabric
Manufacturer:	Carl Beisser GmbH
Product:	stainless steel fabric

Material:	stainless steel
Weave type:	ribbed
Transparency:	close to 0 %
Wire thickness:	warp wire < 1 mm
	weft bar < 1 mm
Usual width:	up to 2 m
Weight:	approx. 3 kg/m²
Manufacturer:	Haver & Boecker
Product:	Stainless steel fabric, "Flexomesh"

Material:	stainless steel
Weave type:	ribbed
Transparency:	close to 0 %
Wire thickness:	warp wire 0.36 mm
	weft bar 0.28 mm
Usual width:	up to 1.25 m
Weight:	approx. kg/m²
Manufacturer:	Carl Beisser GmbH
Product:	Stainless steel fabric

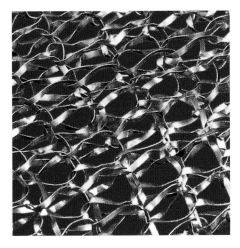

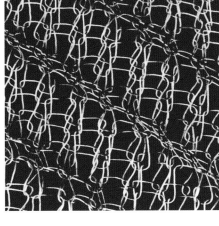

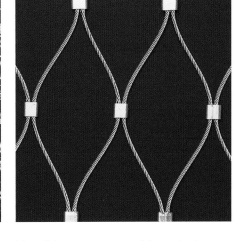

Material:	copper
Weave type:	knitted
Transparency:	as required
Wire thickness:	flat wire
	d = 0.1–0.3 mm
Usual width:	150 mm–1 m
Weight:	approx. 0.077 kg/m²
Mesh width:	as required (filter technology)
Manufacturer:	F. Carl Schröter
Product:	knitted copper wire

Material:	stainless steel
Weave type:	knitted
Transparency:	as required
Wire thickness:	round wire, corrugated
	d = 0.1–0.3 mm,
	300 mm–1 m
Usual width:	
Weight:	approx. 0.236 kg/m²
Mesh width:	as required (filter technology)
Manufacturer:	F. Carl Schröter
Product:	knitted stainless steel

Material:	stainless steel
Weave type:	special: layered
Transparency:	80–98 %
Wire thickness:	round braided cable 7 × 7, d = 1/1.5/2 mm
	round braided cable 7 × 19, d = 3/4 mm
Usual width:	on demand
Weight:	approx. 0.17–2.6 kg/m² according to mesh width
Press collars:	tinned copper
Manufacturer:	Carl Stahl GmbH
Product:	Stainless steel net, "X-Tend"

Suggested literature:

Haselbach, Manfred: Kupfer im Hochbau. Berlin: Deutsches Kupfer-Institut. 1987

Koewius; Gross, Alexander; Angehrn, Gerhard: Aluminium-Konstruktionen. Düsseldorf: Aluminium-Verlag. 1999

Liersch, Klaus: Belüftete Dach- und Wandkonstruktionen, various volumes since 1981. Wiesbaden and Berlin: Bauverlag

Moritz, Karsten: Membranwerkstoffe im Hochbau. In: Detail 6/2000, pp. 1050-1055. Munich: Institut für internationale Architektur-Dokumentation

NN: Beschichten von Kupfer und Kupfer-Zink-Legierungen mit farblosen Transparentlacken. Berlin: Deutsches Kupfer-Institut. 1991

Prouvé, Jean: Meister der Blechumformung, Das neue Blech. Cologne: Verlagsgesellschaft Rudolf Müller GmbH. 1991

Schäfer, Stefan: Neuartige metallische Dacheindeckung. In: Detail 5/2000, pp. 880 – 882. Munich: Institut für internationale Architektur-Dokumentation

Schittich, Christian (ed.): Gebäudehüllen – Konzepte, Schichten, Material. Munich: Institut für internationale Architektur-Dokumentation. 2001

Schulitz, Helmut; Sobek, Werner; Habermann, Karl: Stahlbauatlas neu. Munich: Institut für internationale Architektur-Dokumentation. 1999

Assembly and fixing of metal fabrics

The geometry of facade areas is a major factor in the assembly of metal mesh products. A logical classification could be made by dividing them into planar surfaces, surfaces curved about a single axis, and those curved about two axes. In most cases, the facades to be clad are in the form of flat planes. If flat areas of mesh are pre-tensioned across the surface of a facade, negative effects such as vibration, whipping and flapping can be reduced, but heavy anchoring loads will occur at the points of support. These loads will have to be transmitted to the supporting structure.

In accordance with the load-bearing principles relating to cable structures, plane surfaces cannot transmit loads perpendicularly to the main axis. For this to be possible, the wire axis would have to be curved. Furthermore, the great reaction forces at the supports in the direction of the main axes have to be taken into account. The insertion of springs at the fixing points provides a certain latitude for distortion while still maintaining the requisite tensioning.

Surfaces that are curved about a single axis are relatively easy to realize. Especially in interior situations, where there is no wind to cause flapping, metal fabric can be freely suspended to form soffits or wall linings, for example. The pre-tension then remains low, and the requisite stiffness can be achieved with stronger warp or weft wires. Using mesh sheeting where it will be subject to wind loads requires numerous fixings along the "weak" axis. The principle underlying the manufacture of ribbed weaves, with warp or weft wires of large dimensions, facili-

tates the transmission of loads along a single axis and allows greater distances between fixings. In such cases, the wires act like a series of closely spaced beams subject to bending. The softer wires along the "weak" axis either bear no loads at all or transmit only tension loads.

Areas curved about two axes are the ideal structural solution, since the geometry allows the relevant loads – especially external wind loads – to be transmitted more simply to the supporting structure. To avoid complex cutting and intersections, the appropriate weave, with flexible mesh cross-sections, should be used. The danger of a displacement of the mesh wires can be avoided through correct detailing. Additional constructional elements such as clamping angles and frames, round rods and loops woven into the mesh, projecting warp or weft rods, invisible wire ties and clips, forked fittings, and eye bolts or screws can also be helpful in this context. The principles of constructional jointing relating to the transmission of loads over large areas to avoid peak stresses should obviously be heeded in this respect. Ideal forms of jointing are those that can be post-tensioned and that allow scope for adjustment to achieve an absolutely plane surface. Nor should one forget that fabric mesh products have to be fixed in a hanging state, like curtains. The dead load is then transmitted through the upper supports and conveyed to the ground.

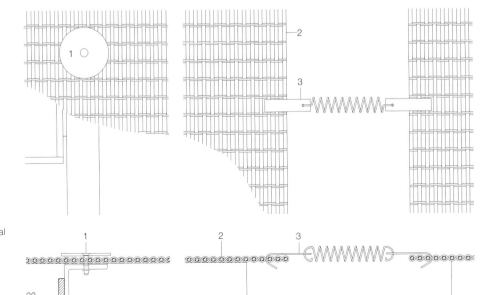

32   Cycling stadium in Berlin
     Top view and section of the bracing of the metal fabric on the roof: scale 1:5
     1 Stainless steel disc Ø 84.3 mm
     2 Stainless steel fabric
     3 Flat steel 110/30/2 mm with helical tension spring Ø 2.8 mm
     Architects: Dominique Perrault, Paris

Regulations · Manufacturers

Glass
Standards

DIN 1249 Glass in building

DIN 1259 Glass (Terminology for glass types and groups)

DIN 1286 Insulating glass units; air filled

DIN 4102 Fire behaviour of building materials and building components

DIN 4108 Thermal insulation in buildings

DIN 4109 Sound insulation in buildings

DIN 4242 Glass block walls; construction and dimensioning

DIN 4701 Regeln für die Berechnung des Wärmebedarfs von Gebäuden (Rules for calculating heating requirements in buildings)

DIN 5036 Radiometric and photometric properties of materials

DIN 6169 Colour rendering

DIN 12 111 Prüfung von Glas, Gießverfahren zur Prüfung der Wasserbeständigkeit von Glas als Werkstoff bei 98 °C und Einteilung der Gläser in hydrolytische Klassen (Testing glass, casting processes for testing the water resistance of glass as a material at 98 °C and dividing glass into hydrolitic classes)

DIN 12 116 Testing of glass – Resistance to attack by a boiling aqueous solution of hydrochloric acid – Method of test and classification

DIN 12 337 Glas im Bauwesen (Glass in building)

DIN 18 054 Fenster, Einbruchhemmende Fenster (Windows, burglar resistant windows)

DIN 18 361 Glazing works

DIN 18 545 Glazing with sealants; rebates; requirements

DIN 52 290 Angriffhemmende Verglasungen (High security glazing)

DIN 52 293 Prüfung von Glas, Prüfung der Glasdichtheit von gasgefülltem Mehrscheiben-Isolierglas (Testing glass, testing the glass seal in gas-filled, multi-layer insulating glass)

DIN 52 338 Methods of testing flat glass for use in buildings; ball drop test on laminated glass

DIN 52 344 Testing of glass; testing the effect of alternating atmosphere on multilayer insulating glass

DIN 52 345 Testing of glass; determination of dew point temperature of insulating glass units; laboratory test

DIN 52 349 Prüfung von Glas, Bruchstruktur von Glas für bauliche Anlagen (Testing glass, fracture structure in building glass)

DIN 52 460 Sealing and glazing – Terms

DIN 52 611 Determination of thermal resistance of building elements

DIN 52 612 Testing of thermal insulating materials; determination of thermal conductivity by the guarded hot plate apparatus

DIN 52 619 Testing of thermal insulation; determination of the thermal resistance and the thermal transmission coefficient of windows; determination on frames

DIN 67 507 Lichttransmissionsgrade, Strahlungstransmissionsgrade und Gesamtenergiedurchlassgrade von Verglasungen (Light transmission efficiency, radiation transmission efficiency and overall energy transmission efficiency in glazing)

DIN EN 356 (E) Glass in building – Security glazing – Testing and classification of resistance against manual attack

DIN EN 572 Glass in building – Basic soda lime silicate glass products

DIN EN 673 (E) Glass in building – Determination of thermal transmittance (U value)

DIN EN 1063 (E) Glass in building – Security glazing – Testing and classification of resistance against bullet attack

DIN EN 1863 (E) Glass in building – Heat strengthened soda lime silicate glass

DIN EN 10 204 Types of inspection documents

DIN EN 12 150 (E) Glass in building – Thermally toughened soda lime silicate safety glass

DIN EN 12 600 Glass in building – Pendulum tests – Impact test method and classification for flat glass

DIN EN ISO 12543 (E) Glass in building – Laminated glass and laminated safety glass

on "Structural gluing":
DIN EN ISO 291: Plastics – Standard atmospheres for conditioning and testing

DIN EN ISO 527: Plastics – Determination of tensile properties

DIN EN 26 922: Adhesives; determination of tensile strength of butt joints

Guidelines:
Verein deutscher Ingenieure – VDI Richtlinien
www.vdi.de

VdS Verband der Sachversicherer e.V. – VdS-Richtlinien
www.vds.de

i.f.t., Institut für Fenstertechnik e. V., Rosenheim
www.ift-rosenheim.de

Hadamar Technische Richtlinien des Instituts des Glaserhandwerks für Verglasungstechnik und Fensterbau, inbesondere:
  Schrift 1 Dichtstoffe für Verglasungen und Anschlussfugen
  Schrift 2 Windlast und Glasdicke
  Schrift 3 Klotzung und Verglasungseinheiten
  Schrift 9 Richtlinien für den Bau und die Verglasung von Metallrahmen-Schaufenstern und gleichartigen Konstruktionen
  Schrift 10 Fachliche begriffe aus dem Berufsbereich des Glashandwerks
  Schrift 11 Montage von Spiegeln
  Schrift 12 Fensterwände, Bemessung und Ausführung, Erläuterungen zu DIN 18056
  Schrift 13 Verglasen mit Dichtprofilen
  Schrift 14 Glas im Bauwesen, Einteilung der Glaserzeugnisse
  Schrift 16 Fenster und Fensterwände für Hallenbäder
  Schrift 17 Verglasen mit Isolierglas
  Schrift 18 Umwehrungen mit Glas
  Schrift 19 Überkopf-Verglasungen
  Schrift 20 Montage von Fenstern

(Hadamar Technical Guidelines from the Institut des Glaserhandwerks für Verglasungstechnik und Fensterbau, particularly: 1 Insulating materials for glazing and jointing 2 Wind load and glass thickness 3 Blocking and glazing units 9 Guidelines for constructing and glazing metal-framed display windows and similar structures 10 Technical terms from the glass industry 11 Fitting mirrors 12 Curtain walls, assessment and execution, explanations of DIN 18056 13 Glazing with sealed units 14 Glass in building, glass product categories 16 Windows and curtain walls for indoor swimming pools 17 Glazing with insulating glass 18 Protection using glass 19 Overhead glazing 20 Fitting windows)

Plastics – sheeting, membranes
Standards

DIN 7728 Kennbuchstaben und Kurzzeichen (Code letters and acronyms)

DIN 16 906 Testing of plastic sheeting and films; sample and specimen preparation and conditioning

DIN 18 032 Halls and rooms for sports and multipurpose use

DIN 18 234 Fire safety of large roofs for buildings – Fire exposure from below

DIN 50 035 Terms and definitions used on ageing of materials; Part 1: Basic terms and definitions Part 2: Examples concerning polymeric materials

DIN 53 350 Testing of plastics films and coated textile fabrics, manufactured using plastics; determination of stiffness in bending, method according to Ohlsen

DIN 53 351 (E) Testing of artificial leather and similar shut materials – Behaviour at permanent folding (Flexometer-method)

DIN 53 354 Testing of artificial leather; tensile test;

DIN 53 356 Testing of artificial leather and similar sheet materials; tear growth test

DIN 53 359 (E) Testing of artificial leather; repeated flexure test

DIN 53 362 (E) Testing of plastics films and textile fabrics (excluding nonwovens), coated or not coated with plastics – Determination of stiffness in bending – Method according to Cantilever

DIN 53 363 (E) Testing of plastic films – Tear test using trapezoidal test specimen with incision

DIN 53 370 (E) Testing of plastic films; determination of the thickness by mechanical feeling

DIN 53 380 Testing of plastics – Determination of gas transmission rate; part 1: volumetrical method for testing of plastic films; part 2: manometric method for testing of plastic films

DIN 53 386 Testing of plastics and elastomers, Exposure to natural weathering

DIN 53 444 Mechanische Eigenschaften, Kriechmodul (Mechanical properties, creep module)

DIN 53 455 Mechanische Eigenschaften, Streckspannung, Dehnung, Zugfestigkeit, Reißdehnung (Mechanical properties, yield point, tensile strain, tensile strength, elongation at break)

DIN 53 457 Mechanische Eigenschaften, Elastizitätsmodul (Mechanical properties, elasticity module)

DIN 53 460 Thermische Eigenschaften, Vicat-Erweichungstemperatur (Thermal properties, Vicat softening temperature)

DIN 53 461 Thermische Eigenschaften, Formbeständigkeitstemperatur (Thermal properties, heat deflection temperature)

DIN 53 515 Determination of tear strength of rubber elastomers and plastic film using Graves angle test piece with nick

DIN 53 530 Testing of organic materials; Separation test on fabric plies bonded together

DIN 53 598-1, Statistical evaluation at off-hand samples with examples from testing of rubbers and plastics

DIN 53 752 Testing of plastics; determination of the coefficient of linear thermal expansion

DIN 60 001 Textile fibres
Part 1: natural fibres and letter codes
Part 2: forms of fibres and manufacturing

DIN EN 1875-3 Rubber- or plastics-coated fabrics – Determination of tear strength – Trapezoidal method

DIN EN ISO 62 Plastics – Determination of water absorption

DIN EN ISO 75 Plastics – Determination of temperature of deflection under load
Part 1: general test method
Part 2: plastics and ebonite
Part 3: high-strength thermosetting laminates and long-fibre-reinforced plastics

DIN EN ISO 175 Plastics – Methods of test for the determination of the effects of immersion in liquid chemicals

DIN EN ISO 291 Plastics – Standard atmospheres for conditioning and testing

DIN EN ISO 305 Plastics – Determination of thermal stability of poly(vinyl chloride), related chlorine-containing homopolymers and copolymers and their compounds – Discoloration method

DIN EN ISO 306 Plastics – Thermoplastic materials – Determination of Vicat softening temperature

DIN EN ISO 527 Plastics – Determination of tensile properties

DIN EN ISO 846 Plastics – Evaluation of the action of microorganisms

DIN EN ISO 899 Plastics – Determination of creep behaviour
Part 1: Tensile creep
Part 2: Flexural creep by three-point loading

DIN EN ISO 1043 Plastics - Symbols and abbreviated terms
Part 1: Basic polymers and their special characteristics
Part 2: Fillers and reinforcing materials
Part 3: Plasticizers
Part 4: Flame retardants

DIN EN ISO 2286 Rubber- or plastics-coated fabrics – Determination of roll characteristics
Part 1: Method for determination of the length, width and net mass
Part 2: Methods for determination of total mass per unit area, mass per unit area of coating and mass per unit area of substrate
Part 3: Method for determination of thickness

DIN EN ISO 2578 Plastics – Determination of time-temperature limits after prolonged exposure to heat

DIN EN ISO 9237 Textiles – Determination of permeability of fabrics to air

Metal
Standards
DIN 1055-2 Design Loads for Buildings; soil Characteristics; specific weight, angle of friction, cohesion, angle of wall friction

DIN 1751 Bleche und Blechstreifen aus Kupfer und Kupfer-Knetlegierungen, kaltgewalzt, Maße (Sheet and strip in copper and wrought copper alloys)

DIN 1787 Kupfer, Halbzeug (Copper, semi-finished)

DIN 4102 Fire behaviour of building materials and building components

DIN 4108 Thermal insulation in buildings

DIN 4109 Sound insulation in buildings; requirements and testing

DIN 9430 Aerospace; sampling of semi-finished products in light metals; wrought aluminium alloys, titanium and titanium alloys

DIN 17 744 Wrought nickel alloys with molybdenum and chromium – Chemical composition

DIN 17 860 Titanium and titanium alloy plate, sheet and strip; technical delivery conditions

DIN 17 863 Titanium wire

DIN 17 869 Material properties of titanium and titanium alloys; additional data

DIN 18 202 Dimensional tolerances in building construction – Buildings

DIN 18 339 Contract procedures for building works – Part C: general technical specifications for building works; Sheet metal works

DIN 18 351 Contract procedures for building works – Part C: general technical specifications for building works; facade works

DIN 18 516 Cladding for externals walls, ventilated at rear

DIN 24 041 Perforated plates – Dimensions

DIN 24 537 Flooring grids

DIN 50 923 (E) Electroplated coatings – Duplex coatings of zinc or zinc alloy coatings with organic coatings on iron or steel

DIN 50 939 Corrosion protection – Chromating of aluminium – Principles and methods of test

DIN 50 959 Electrodeposited coatings; corrosive resistance of electrodeposited coatings on iron and steel under different climatic conditions

DIN 50 961 Electroplated coatings – Zinc coatings on iron and steel - Terms, testing and corrosion resistance

DIN EN 485 Aluminium and aluminium alloys; sheet, strip and plate

DIN EN 611 Tin and tin alloys – Pewter and pewterware

DIN EN 988 Zinc and zinc alloys – Specification for rolled flat products for building

DIN EN 1172 Copper and copper alloys – Sheet and strip for building purposes

DIN EN 1179 Zinc and zinc alloys – Primary zinc

DIN EN 1652 Copper and copper alloys – Plate, sheet, strip and circles for general purposes

DIN EN 10 020 Definition and classification of grades of steel

DIN EN 10 088 Stainless steels

DIN EN 10 240 Internal and/or external protective coatings for steel tubes – Specification for hot dip galvanized coatings applied in automatic plants

DIN EN 10 147 Continuously hot-dip zinc coated structural steel strip and sheet – Technical delivery conditions

DIN EN 13 658 (E) Metal lath and beads – Definitions, requirements and test methods

DIN EN 14 509 (E) Self-supporting double skin metal faced insulating sandwich panels – Factory made products – Specification

DIN EN 29 453 Soft solder alloys; chemical compositions and forms

DIN EN ISO 1461 Hot dip galvanized coatings on fabricated iron and steel articles – Specifications and test methods

DIN EN ISO 4526 (E) Metallic coatings - Electroplated coatings of nickel and nickel alloys for engineering purposes

DIN EN ISO 6158 Metallic coatings – Electrodeposited coatings of chromium for engineering purposes

DIN EN ISO 9044 Industrial woven wire cloth – Technical requirements and testing

DIN ISO 3310 Test sieves – Technical requirements and testing

DIN ISO 4782 Metal wire for industrial wire screens and woven wire cloth

DIN ISO 4783 Industrial wire screens and woven wire cloth – Guide to the choice of aperture size and wire diameter combinations

DIN ISO 9044 Industrial woven wire cloth – Technical requirements and testing

LN 1791 Coiled and flat strips from copper and copper alloys; cold rolled, dimensions

Guidelines:
ISO 565 Test sieves – Metal wire cloth, perforated metal plate and electroformed sheet – Nominal sizes of openings

RAL-RG 681 Güte- und Prüfbestimmungen für Titanzink und Bauelemente aus Titanzink (Quality and testing for titanium zinc and titanium zinc building elements)

Richtlinien für die Ausführung von Metall-Dächern, Außenwandbekleidungen und Bauklempner-Arbeiten – Entwurf (Fachregeln des Klempner-Handwerks) des Zentralverbandes Sanitär-Heizung Klima e. V. (Guidelines for constructing metal roofs, external wall cladding and structural plumbing (technical plumbing regulations) from the Zentralverband Sanitär-Heizung Klima e. V.)

Glass – list of manufacturers

Generally speaking the products given in brackets represent only part of a firm's wider product range.

BGT Bischoff Glastechnik AG
Alexanderstraße 2
D–75015 Bretten
Tel.: +49 7252 503-0
Fax: +49 7252 503-283
www.bgt-bretten.de
(Flat glass processing and finishing, fire retardant glass)

COLT International (Schweiz) AG
Ruessenstraße 5
CH–6340 Baar
Tel.: +41 41 7685454
Fax: +41 41 7685455
www.coltinfo.ch
(Daylight technology, sunshading)

Corning GmbH
- Corning International
Abraham-Lincoln Straße 30
D–65189 Wiesbaden
Tel.: +49 611 7366-142
Fax: +49 611 7366-143
www.corning.com
(Light-sensitive glass, LCD)

CRICURSA Polígono Industrial Coll
de La Manya
E–08400 Granollers/Barcelona
Tel. Head office: +34 93 8404470
Tel. International: +34 93 8404472
www.cricursa.com
(Curved glass, safety glass)

Dorma Glas GmbH
Max-Planck-Straße 37-43
D–32107 Bad Salzuflen
Tel.: +49 5222 924-0
Fax: +49 5222 21009
www.dorma.de
(Glass for doors, lobbies)

DuPont de Nemours GmbH
Du Pont Straße 1
D–61343 Bad Homburg
Tel.: +49 6172 87-0
Fax: +49 6172 87-1500
www.dupont.com/safetyglass
(Laminated glass products)

Eckelt Glas GmbH
Resthofstraße 18
A–4400 Steyr
Tel.: +43 7252 894-0
Fax: +43 7252 894-24
www.eckelt.at
(System products for facades, fully etched float glass)

emdelight GmbH
Ottostraße 7
D–50859 Köln
Tel.: +49 2234 6905-0
Fax: +49 2234 6905-28
www.emdelight.de
(Edge-lit glass with LEDs)

FLABEG Holding GmbH
Auf der Reihe 2
D–45884 Gelsenkirchen
Tel.: +49 209-94799-0
Fax: +49 209-94799-98
www.flabeg.com
(Solar systems, safety glass)

Flachglas MarkenKreis GmbH
Auf der Reihe 2
D–45884 Gelsenkirchen
Tel.: +49 209 91329-0
Fax: +49 209 91329-29
www.flachglas-markenkreis.de
(Glass for thermal insulation, sunshading, sound insulation and safety purposes)

Glas Conzelmann
Flachglasveredelung
Weidenweg 43
D–72336 Balingen
Tel.: +49 7433 304-0
Fax: +49 7433 304-33
www.glasconzelmann.de
www.consafis.de
(Insulating glass)

Franz Mayer'sche Hofkunstanstalt
GmbH
Seidlstraße 25
D–80335 München
Tel.: +49 89 545962-0
Fax: +49 89 593346
www.mayersche-hofkunst.de
(Glass design, printing, painting and mosaic)

Gesimat GmbH
Köpenicker Straße 325
D–12555 Berlin
Tel.: +49 30 6576-2609
Fax: +49 30 6576-2608
www.gesimat.de
(Electrochromic glass development)

GLASFISCHER
Gottlieb-Daimler-Straße 46-48
D–71711 Murr
Tel.: +49 7144 8263-0
Fax: +49 7144 8263-33
www.glasfischer.de
(3-pane glazing with sheeting)

glas platz
Auf den Pühlen 5
D–51674 Wiehl-Bomig
Tel.: +49 2261 7890-0
Fax: +49 2261 7890-10
www.glas-platz.de
(LED coated glass)

Glas Schuler GmbH & Co. KG
Ziegelstraße 23-25
D–91126 Rednitzhembach
Tel.: +49 9122 9756-0
Fax: +49 9122 9756-40
www.isolette.com
(Insulating glass with built-in blind)

Glas Trösch AG
Hy-Tech-Glass
Industriestraße 12
CH–4922 Bützberg
Tel.: +41 629585400
Fax: +41 629585394
www.glastroesch.ch
(Facade systems, interior fitting, thermal insulation glass, non-reflecting glass)

GLASBAU HAHN GmbH & Co. KG
Hanauer Landstraße 211
D–60314 Frankfurt/M.
Tel.: +49 69 94417-0
Fax: +49 69 49901-51
www.glasbau-hahn.de
(Louvred windows)

Glasfabrik Lamberts
GmbH & Co. KG
Postfach 560
D–95624 Wunsiedel
Tel.: +49 9232 605-0
Fax: +49 9232 605-33
www.lambertsglas.com
(Profile, ornamental glass)

Glaswerke Arnold GmbH & Co. KG
Alfred-Klingele-Straße 15
D–73630 Remshalden
Tel.: +49 7151 7096-0
Fax: +49 7151 7096-90
www.glaswerke-arnold.de
(Glass for thermal insulation, sunshading, sound insulation, fire protection)

Glaverbel, Belgien
represented in Germany by:
- Bluhm & Plate GmbH
Von-Bronsart-Straße 14
D–22885 Barsbüttel
Tel.: +49 40 670884-0
Fax: +49 40 670884-10
-Schlatt
Robert Bosch-Straße 36
D–46397 Bocholt
Tel.: +49 2871 99400

Fax: +49 2871 183681
www.glaverbel.com
(Wide range of products)

HT Troplast AG
Mühlheimer Straße 26
D-53840 Troisdorf
Tel.: +49 2241 85-0
Fax: +49 2241 85-2793
www.ht-troplast.com
www.trosifol.com
(Sheeting for coating glass)

Innotec-Gruppe, group of 5 glass
manufacturers, e.g.:
Glas Engels GmbH
Karl Legien Straße 2
D–45356 Essen
Tel.: +49 201 83496-00
Fax: +49 201 83496-35
www.innotec-gruppe.de
(Tempered safety glass, laminated glass, bullet-proof glass, walk-on glass, enamelled glass, insulating glass)

PD-Interglas Technologies AG
Benzstraße 14
D–89155 Erbach
Tel.: +49 7305 955-0
Fax: +49 7305 955-513
www.interglas-technologies.com
(Glass fabrics, printed circuit materials)

Interpane Glas Industrie AG
Sohnreystraße 21
D–37697 Lauenförde
Tel.: +49 5273 809-0
Fax: +49 5273 88263
www.interpane.net
(Glass finishers, glass for sound insulation, insulation, thermal and safety purposes)

ISOCLIMA S.p.A.
via A. Volta, 14
I–35042 Este
Tel.: +39 0429 4188
Fax: +39 0429 3878
www.isoclima.net
(Chemically tempered glass)

Joel Berman Glass Studios Ltd,
1-1244 Cartwright Street
CDN–Vancouver BC V6H 3R8
Tel.: +1 888 505 4527 (GLASS)
In Vancouver. 604.684.8332
Fax.+1 604 684 8373
www.jbermanglass.com
(Glass textures, corrugated glass)

Luxaclair® Sealed Glass Blinds, NL
Lizenznehmer in Deutschland:
Glaszentrum G.F. Schweikert GmbH
Salzstraße 191
D–74076 Heilbronn
Tel.: +49 7131 130-0
Fax: +49 7131 130-119
www.luxaclair.co.uk
www.glaszentrum-schweikert.de
(Integrated sunshading)

Okalux GmbH
Am Jöspshecklein 1
D–97828 Marktheidenfeld
Tel.: +49 9391 900-0
Fax: +49 9391 900-100
www.okalux.de
(Insulating glass with various inlays,
TWD, light pitcher)

Parabeam b.v.
P.O. Box 134
NL–5700 AC Helmond
Tel.: +31 492 591222
Fax: +31 492 591220
www.parabeam3d.com
(3D fibre-glass structures)

Pilkington Deutschland AG
- Basic glass:
Alfredstraße 236
D–45133 Essen
Tel.: +49 201 125-5312
Fax: +49 201 125-5099
- Fire protection glass, bullet-proof
glass:
Haydnstraße 19
D–45884 Gelsenkirchen
Tel.: +49 209 168-2135
Fax: +49 209 168-2026
- Profile glass:
Bauglasindustrie GmbH
Hüttenstraße 33
D–66839 Schmelz
Tel.: +49 6887 303-21
Fax: +49 6887 303-45
www.pilkington.de
www.pilkington.com
(Wide product range)

Saint-Gobain Glass Deutschland
GmbH
Victoriaallee 3-5
D–52066 Aachen
Tel.: +49 241 516-2002
Fax: +49 241 516-2003
www.saint-gobain-glass.com
(Wide product range)

Saint-Gobain Oberland AG
Division Bauglas
Siemensstraße 1
D–56422 Wirges
Tel.: +49 2602 681-0
Fax: +49 2602 681-425

www.solaris-glasstein.de
(Glass blocks)

Schollglas GmbH
Schollstraße 4
D–30890 Barsinghausen
Tel.: +49 5105 777-0
Fax: +49 5105 777-118
www.schollglas.de
(Flat glass of all kinds, glass con-
struction)

Schott Glas
Hattenbergstraße 16
D–55122 Mainz
Tel.: +49 6131 66-0
Fax: +49 6131 66-2000
www.schott.de
www.schott.com
(Wide product range)
- Glass tubes:
Schott Rohrglas GmbH
Erich-Schott-Straße 14
D–95666 Mitterteich
Tel.: +49 9633 80-0
Fax: +49 9633 80-614
www.schott.com/rohrglas
(Tubes for solar energy conversion,
laminated glass tubes)
- Special glass:
SCHOTT Special Flat Glass
A Business Segment of
Schott Spezialglas GmbH
Hüttenstraße1
D–31073 Grünenplan
Tel.: +49 5187 771-0
Fax: +49 5187 771-300
www.schott.com/desag
(Special glass, LED)

Siteco Beleuchtungstechnik GmbH
Ohmstraße 50
D–83301 Traunreut
Tel.: +49 8669 33-0
Fax: +49 8669 33-397
www.siteco.de
(Interior and exterior lighting, day-
light systems)

Solutia Inc., USA
Sales in Germany
CP Films Vertriebs GmbH
Herforder Straße 119-131
D–33609 Bielefeld
Tel.: +49 521 93248-0
Fax: +49 52193248-28
www.solutia.com
www.vanceva.com
(PVB and metal sheeting for lami-
nated glass)

Southwall Europe GmbH
Southwallstraße 1
D–01900 Großröhrsdorf
Tel.: +49 1149 35952-440

Fax: +49 1149 35952-44320
www.southwalleurope.de
www.southwall.com
(Special thermal insulation sheeting
for absorption insulation, reflection)

STEINDL GLAS GmbH
Gries 303
A–6361 Itter
Tel.: +43 5335 3900
Fax: +43 5335 3900-35
www.steindlglas.com
(Fire protection glass, facade
systems, insulating glass)

Tambest Oy
Lasikaari 1
FIN–33960 Pirkkala
Tel.: +358 3 31323-000
Fax: +358 3 31323-350
www.tambest.fi
www.glasrobots.fi
(Curved insulating glass)

VEGLA Vereinigte Glaswerke GmbH
(taken over by Saint-Gobain Glass,
q.v.)
(Thermal insulation glass)

Vetroarredo s.p.a
Via Reginaldo Giuliani, 360
I–50141 c.a.p. Florenz
Tel.: +39 055 44951
Fax: +39 055 455295
www.vetroarredo.com
(Glass blocks)

3M Deutschland GmbH
Carl-Schurz-Straße 1
D–41453 Neuss
Tel.: +49 2131 14-0
Fax: +49 2131 14-2649
www.3m.com
(Optical sheeting, special sheeting)

Links/addresses:

Baustoffsammlung der Fakultät für
Architektur der TU München
Theresienstraße 92
Contact: Johann Weber
Tel.: +49 89 289-22354
Opening times differ,
appointments possible
Internet: wdb.ebb1.arch.tu-
muenchen.de/glas.php

Bundesverband Flachglas e.V.
Mühlheimer Straße 1
D–53840 Troisdorf
Tel.: +49 2241 8727-0
Fax: +49 2241 8727-10
www.bf-flachgasverband.de

Deutsche Glastechnische
Gesellschaft e.V. (DGG) &
Hüttentechnische Vereinigung
der Deutschen Glasindustrie e.V.
(HVG)
Siemensstraße 45
63071 Offenbach
Tel.: +49 69 975861-0
Fax: +49 69 975861-99
www.hvg-dgg.de

Fraunhofer-Institut für
Silicatforschung ISC
Neunerplatz 2
D–97082 Würzburg
Tel.: +49 931 4100-0
Fax: +49 931 4100-199
www.isc.fraunhofer.de

glasstec - Internationale Fachmesse
für Neuheiten aus Glasmaschinen-
bau, Glasherstellung- und -verede-
lung sowie Glaserhandwerk,
Internetportal
www.glasstec.de

Institut für Fenstertechnik e.V.
Rosenheim
Theodor-Gietl-Straße 7-9
D–83026 Rosenheim
Tel.: +49 8031 261-0
Fax: +49 8031 261-290
www.ift-rosenheim.de

Material ConneXion Milano
c/o Fiera Milano
Piazzale Giulio Cesare
I–20145 Mailand
Tel.: +39 0243981128
Fax: +39 0248022992
www.materialconnexion.com
(Data base for new materials)

VDI Verein Deutscher Ingenieure
e.V., Düsseldorf
Portal für Ingenieure
www.vdi.de

Plastic / semi-finished sheeting products – List of manufacturers

Generally speaking the products given in brackets represent only part of a firm's wider product range.

ABET GmbH
Füllenbruchstraße 189 H-K
D–32051 Herford
Tel.: +49 5221 3477-0
Fax: +49 5221 33196
www.abet.de
(HPL decorative panels)

Arla Plast AB
Box 33
S–59030 Borensberg
Tel.: +46 141 203800
Fax: +46 141 41430
www.arlaplast.se
(Polycarbonate)

Barlo Plastics
Leukaard 1
B–2440 Geel
Tel.: +49 5225 87 33 994
Fax: +49 5225 87 33 995
www.barloplastics.com
(PMMA, PC, PETG, PS, SAN)

BASF Schweiz AG
CH–8820 Wädenswil
Tel.: +41 17819111
Fax: +41 17819388
www.basf.ch
(Aerogel etc.)

BOMIN SOLAR GmbH
Industriestraße 8-10
D–79541 Lörrach
Tel.: +49 7621 95960
Fax: +49 7621 54368
www.bomin-solar.de
(Light control)

Brakel Aero GmbH
Alte Hünxer Straße 179
D–46562 Voerde
Tel.: +49 281 404-0
Fax: +49 281 404-99
www.brakel-aero.de
www.grillodur.de
(GRP, PC, light elements)

Butzbach GmbH Industrietore
Robert-Bosch-Straße 4
D–89257 Illertissen
Tel.: +49 7303 951-0
Fax: +49 7303 951-470
www.butzbach.com
(GRP facade systems)

Cabot GmbH
Josef-Bautz-Straße 15
D–63457 Hanau
Tel.: +49 6181 505-191
Fax: +49 6181 505-201
www.wdk.de/cabot.htm
(Aerogel)

Color Change Corporation
1545 Burgundy Parkway
US–60107 Streamwood, IL
Tel.: +1 630 289-0900
Fax: +1 630 289-0909
www.colorchange.com
(Thermochromic and photochromic plastics)

CTS Composites Technologie
Systeme GmbH
Mercatorstaße 43
D–21502 Geesthacht
Tel.: +49 4152 8885-0
Fax: +49 4152 8885-55
www.ctscom.de
(GRP units, gratings)

Fiberline Composites A/S
Nr. Bjertvej 88
DK–6000 Kolding
Tel.: +45 70 137713
Fax: +45 70 137714
www.fiberline.com
(GRP, gratings)

General Electric Plastics
Eisenstraße 5
D–65428 Rüsselsheim
Tel.: +49 61426010
Fax: +49 614265746
www.geplastics.com
(Hollow cellular sheeting with printed stripes)

Gutta Werke GmbH
Bahnhofstraße 51-57
D–77746 Schutterwald
Tel.: +49 781 609-0
Fax: +49 781 609-600
www.gutta.com
(Tongue and groove hollow cellular sheeting)

Hahlbrock GmbH
Wischhöfers Weg 6-7
D–31515 Wunstorf
Tel.: +49 5033 938-0
Fax: +49 5033 938-21
www.halbrock.de
(GRP, curved panels)

Ing. R. Zeiler GmbH
Simonystraße 22
A–5550 Radstadt
Tel.: +43 6452 6510
Fax: +43 6452 6642

www.zeiler.at
(Shaped thermoplastics)

Jean de Giacinto
Architecture et Composittes
19, rue du Général Mangin
F-33200 Bordeaux
Tel.: +33 5 56087871
Fax: +33 5 56085422
(GRP decorative panels)

KaysersbergPlastics
BP No. 27
F–68240 Kaysersberg
Tel.: +33 3 89783230
Fax: +33 3 89471856
www.kaysersberg-plastics.com
(Tongue and groove hollow cellular sheeting)

Lucite International Trading Ltd,
Niederlassung Deutschland
Birkenwaldstraße 38
D–63179 Obertshausen
Tel.: +49 6104 6681-0
Fax: +49 6104 6681-50
www.perspex.co.uk
(PMMA translucent)

Makroform GmbH
Dolivostraße
D–64293 Darmstadt
Tel.: +49 6151 183900-0
Fax: +49 6151 183900-7
www.makroform.com
(PC, PET, PETG)

MKS Kunststoffe
Dritteneimerweg 22
D–56076 Koblenz
Tel.: +49 261 133803
Fax: +49 261 9733831
www.arlaplast.se
(Sales for Arla Plast)

OKALUX GmbH
D–97828 Marktheidenfeld
Tel.: +49 9391 900-0
Fax: +49 9391 900-100
www.okalux.de
(TWD, light control)

Otto Wolff GmbH
Hans-Günther-Sohl-Straße 1
D–40235 Düsseldorf
Tel.: +49 211 967-12
Fax: +49 211 967-7164
www.otto-wolff.com
(Sales for semi-finished plastics)

Panelite
600 Broadway Suite 4c
US–10012 New York, NY
Tel.: +1 212 3430995
Fax: +1 212 3438187

www.e-panelite.com
(Honeycomb panels)

Polyù International S.r.l.
Via Turati, 60
I–20010 Arluno
Tel.: +39 02 90379067
Fax: +39 02 90376965
www.polyu.com
www.sistemapolystar.com
(Tongue and groove hollow cellular sheeting, corrugated hollow cellular sheeting)

RODECA GmbH
Freiherr-vom-Stein-Straße 165
D–45473 Mülheim
Tel.: +49 208 76502-0
Fax: +49 208 76502-11
www.rodeca.de
(Coloured hollow cellular sheeting, tongue and groove)

Röhm GmbH & Co. KG,
Geschäftsbereich Plexiglas
Kirschenallee
D–64293 Darmstadt
Tel.: +49 6151 18-3621
Fax: +49 6151 18-3629
www.roehm.com
www.plexistyle.de
(PMMA, wide range available)

Scobalit AG
Im Hölderli 26
CH–8405 Winterthur
Tel.: +41 52 2352351
Fax: +41 52 2352359
www.scobalit.ch
(GRP panels with special filling)

Simona AG
Teichweg 16
D–55606 Kirn
Tel.: +49 6752 14-0
Fax: +49 6752 14-211
www.simona.de
(PVC UV-stable, PETG UV-stable)

Siteco Beleuchtungstechnik GmbH
Ohmstraße 50
D–83301 Traunreut
Tel.: +49 8669 33-0
Fax: +49 8669 33-397
www.siteco.de
(Lighting technology)

SolarActiveTM International Inc.
18740 Oxnard Street
CDN–91356 #315 Tarzana,
Tel.: +1 818 996-8690
Fax: +1 818 996-8172
www.solaractiveintl.com
(Thermochromic plastics)

Membranes – List of manufacturers

Steba AG
Talstraße 33
CH–8808 Pfäffikon
Tel.: +41 55 4104450
Fax: +41 55 4104083
www.stebakunststoffe.ch
(Sales for hollow cellular sheeting)

Sto AG
Ehrenbachstraße 1
D–79780 Stühlingen
Tel.: +49 7744 57-0
Fax: +49 7744 57-2178
www.sto.de
(TWD rendering)

Links, addresses:

Technical information for the plastics
industry, internet portal
www.kunststoffweb.de

Gesamtverband Kunststoff-verarbei-
tende Industrie e.V.
Am Hauptbahnhof 12
D–60329 Frankfurt/M.
Tel.: +49 69 2710520
Fax: +49 69 232799
www.gkv.de

IBK Darmstadt
Institut für das Bauen mit Kunst-
stoffen e.V.
Mittermayerweg 65
D–64289 Darmstadt
Tel.: +49 6151 48097
Fax: +49 6151 421101
www.ibk-darmstadt.de

Polytronik, press information on
technical uses for electically and
optically active polymers
www.polytronik.fhg.de

Süddeutsches Kunststoff-Zentrum
Frankfurter Straße 15-17
D–97082 Würzburg
Tel.: +49 931 4104-0
Fax.: +49 931 4104-177
www.skz.de

Verband Kunststofferzeugende
Industrie e.V.
Karlstraße 21
D–60329 Frankfurt/M.
Tel.: +49 69 2556-1303
Fax.: +49 69 251060
www.vke.de

B&O Hightex GmbH
Hochstätt 12
D–83253 Rimsting
Tel.: +49 8054 9029-0
Fax: +49 8054 9029-25
www.bo-hightex.de
(Planning, production, execution)

Best-Hall Oy
Yhdystie 3-7
FIN–68300 Kälviä
Tel.: +358 6 8325000
Fax: +358 6 8350477
www.besthall.com
(Tarpaulin covering for large roof areas)

Birdair Europe Stromeyer GmbH
Marlene-Dietrich-Straße 5
D–89231 Neu-Ulm
Tel.: +49 731 98588-765
Fax: +49 731 98588-769
www.birdair.com
(Planning, production, execution)

Buitink Zeilmakerij Duiven
Nieuwgraaf 210
NL–6921 RR Duiven
Tel.: +31 263194-181
Fax: +31 263194-191
www.buitink-technology.com
(Air cushion roofs in ETFE sheeting,
tensioned membrane structures)

Ceno Tec GmbH
Am Eggenkamp 14
D–48268 Greven
Tel.: +49 2571 969-0
Fax: +49 2571 3300
www.ceno-tec.de
(Textile structures)

covertex GmbH
Berghamer Str. 19
D–83119 Obing
Tel.: +49 8624 8969-0
Fax: +49 8624 8969-20
www.covertex.de
(Execution)

DuPont de Nemours GmbH
Du Pont Straße 1
D–61343 Bad Homburg
Tel.: +49 6172 87-0
Fax: +49 6172 87-1500
www.dupont.com
(Basic chemicals for membranes)

FERRARI S.A.
B.P. 54
F–38352 La Tour du Pin, Cedex
Tel.: +33 47497-4133
Fax: +33 47497-6720
www.ferrari-textiles.com
(Composite membranes and
materials)

Festo AG & Co. KG
Ruiter Straße 82
D–73734 Esslingen
Tel.: +49 711 347-0
Fax: +49 711 347-2144
www.festo.de
(Pneumatic structures)

Foiltec GmbH
Steinacker 3
D–28717 Bremen
Tel.: +49 421 69351-0
Fax: +49 421 69351-19
www.foiltec.de
(Transparent roof sheeting)

IPL Ingenieurplanung Leichtbau GmbH
Kapellenweg 2b
D–78315 Radolfzell
Tel.: +49 7732 9464-0
Fax: +49 7732 9464-94
www.ipl-team.de
(Planning for light-weight plate
members, wide roofs)

Koch Membranen GmbH
Nordstraße1
D–83253 Rimsting
Tel.: +49 8051 6909-80
Fax: +49 8051 6909-19
www.kochmembranen.de
(Membrane roofs)

Land Engineering (Scotland) Limited
Gardrum House, Fenwick
GB–Ayrshire KA3 6AS
Tel.: +44 1560 600811
Fax: +44 1560 600818
www.landengineering.co.uk
(Construction, planning)

Nowofol GmbH
Breslauer Straße 15
D–83313 Siegsdorf
Tel.: +49 8662 6602-0
Fax: +49 8662 6602-50
www.nowofol.de
(ETFE sheeting)

Posselt Consult
Ing. techn. Planungsges. mbH
Greimelstr. 26
D–83236 Übersee
Tel.: +49 8642 5970-0
Fax: +49 8642 5970-29
www.posselt-consult.de
(Realizing membrane structures)

Schilgen GmbH & Co.
Gutenbergstraße 1
D–48282 Emsdetten
Tel.: +49 2572 9874-0
Fax: +49 2572 9874-61
www.schilgen.de
(Technical fabrics)

SH Structures Ltd
Moor Lane Trading Estate,
Sherburn-in-Elmet, North Yorkshire
GB–LS25 6ES
Tel.: +44 1977 681931
Fax: +44 1977 681930
www.shstructures.com

Skyspan Europe GmbH
Nordstraße10
D–83253 Rimsting
Tel.: +49 8051 6888-0
Fax: +49 8051 6888-290
www.skyspan.com
(Planning, production, execution)

Taiyo Kogyo Corporation
4-8-4, KigawahigashiYodogawa-Ku
J–Osaka, 532-0012
Tel.: +81 6 6306-3071
Fax: +81 6 6306-3164
www.taiyokogyo.co.jp
(Planning, production, execution)

Toray Deutschland GmbH
Hugenottenallee 175
D–63263 Neu-Isenburg
Tel.: +49 6102 7999-0
Fax: +49 6102 7999-291
www.toray.de
(ETFE sheeting by extrusion)

Verseidag-Indutex GmbH
Industriestraße 56
D–47803 Krefeld
Tel.: +49 2151 876-0
Fax: +49 2151 876-392
www.vsindutex.de
(Development and production)

3M Deutschland GmbH
Carl-Schurz-Straße 1
D–41453 Neuss
Tel.: +49 2131 14-0
Fax: +49 2131 14-2649
www.3m.com
(Polymers for membranes)

Links/addresses:

Lightstructures.de
Leichtbau-Internetportal
www.lightstructures.de

TECHTEXTIL
Forum für technische Textilien und
Vliesstoffe
www.techtextil.com

TensiNet
The European Commission's Com-
munication Network for Tensile
Structures in Europe
www.tensinet.com

Metal – List of manufacturers

Generally speaking the products
given in brackets represent only part
of a firm's wider product range.

AiM Architektur in Metall
EUROSLOT GmbH
Bergstraße 5
D–72622 Nürtingen
Tel.: +49 7022 47460
Fax: +49 7022 45260
www.architektur-in-metall.de
(Stainless steel metal structures)

August Baumeister GmbH + Co.
Industriestraße 58
D–70565 Stuttgart
Tel.: +49 711 78903-0
Fax: +49 711 78903-39
www.baumeister-draht.de
(Wire netting, wire grids,
metal fabric)

BeisserMetall Carl Beisser GmbH
Weilemer Straße 43–47
D–71106 Magstadt
Tel.: +49 7159 4098-0
Fax: +49 7159 4098-11
www.beissermetall.de
(Metal fabric)

bode gmbh
Friedrich-Ebert-Straße 12
D–58730 Fröndenberg
Tel.: +49 2378 9186-0
Fax: +49 2378 9186-13
www.bodegmbh.de
(Preforated sheeting, expanded
metal)

Bückmann GmbH
Sieb- und Separationstechnik
Konstantinstraße 46
D–41238 Mönchengladbach
Tel.: +49 2166 9834-0
Fax: +49 2166 9834-11
www.bueckmann.com
(Metal fabric, grids)

Carl Stahl GmbH
Postweg 41
D–73079 Süssen
Tel.: +49 7162 4007-0
Fax: +49 7162 4007-144
www.carlstahl.com
(Steel cable nets)

Dillinger Fabrik Gelochter Bleche
GmbH
Franz-Meguin-Straße 20
D–66763 Dillingen
Tel.: +49 6831 7003-0
Fax: +49 6831 704076
www.dfgb.de
(Perforated sheeting)

D.O.H. Drahtwerk Oberndorfer Hütte
Oberndorfer Hütte 1
D–35606 Solms-Oberndorf
Tel.: +49 6442 9350-0
Fax: +49 6442 9350-50
www.doh-drahterzeugnisse.de
(Metal fabric for conveyor and
production belts)

Dorstener Drahtwerke
H.W. Brune & Co. GmbH
Marler Straße 109
D–46282 Dorsten
Tel.: +49 2362 2099-0
Fax: +49 2362 26395
www.dorstener-drahtwerke.de

EBENER Fassaden-Profiltechnik
GmbH
Industriegebiet Eichenstruth
D–56470 Bad Marienberg
Tel.: +49 2661 9140-0
Fax: +49 2661 9140-10
www.ebener.de
(Embossed sheeting)

Ernst Meck
Fuggerstraße 16
D–90439 Nürnberg
Tel.: +49 911 27065-0
Fax: +49 911 27065-50
www.ernst-meck.de
(Perforated sheeting)

F. CARL SCHRÖTER
Borstelmannsweg 109-115
D–20537 Hamburg
Tel.: +49 40 219000-0
Fax: +49 40 219000-21
www.fcarlschroeter.de
(Metal fabric, knitted wire, expanded
grids, perforated sheeting)

Heinrich Fiedler GmbH & Co. KG
Weidener Straße 9
D–93059 Regensburg
Tel.: +49 941 6401-0
Fax: +49 941 62414
www.fiedler.de
(Perforating technology, perforated
sheeting)

Franz Fahl GmbH
Lindenstraße 64-66
D–58256 Ennepetal
Tel.: +49 2333 9797-0
Fax: +49 2333 9797-97
www.fahl-lochbleche.de
(Perforated sheeting)

Gantois
B.P. 307
F–88105 St-Dié-des-Vosges Cédex
Tel.: +33 3 2955-2143
Fax: +33 3 2955-3729
www.gantois.com
(Metal fabric, perforated sheeting)

GKD Gebr. Kufferath AG
Metallweberstraße 46
D–52353 Düren
Tel.: +49 2421 803-0
Fax: +49 2421 803-211
www.gkd.de
(Metal fabric)

Gondrexon Industrie N.V.-S.A.
Airport Ring Center, Azalealaan 22
B–1930 Zaventem
Tel.: +32 2 7206060
Fax: +32 2 7250805
www.gondrexon.com
(Wire fabric, expanded grids)

Graepel-STUV GmbH
Waldemar-Estel-Straße 7
D–39615 Seehausen/Altmark
Tel.: +49 39386 27-0
Fax: +49 39386 27-180
www.graepel.de
(Perforated sheeting, sheet-metal
grids)

Haver & Boecker
Drahtweberei und Maschinenfabrik
Carl-Haver-Platz
D–59282 Oelde
Tel.: +49 2522 30-0
Fax: +49 2522 30-403
www.haverboecker.com

Industrie Longhi, Italien
vertreten in Deutschland durch:
Handelsvertetung Heinz Knoche
Birkenhöfe Bitzfeld 1
D–74626 Bretzfeld
Tel.: +49 7946 95717
Fax: +49 7946 95719
www.handelsvertretung-knoche.de
www.italfim.it
www.fils.it
(Expanded grids)

INOX-COLOR GmbH & Co. KG
Industriegebiet Walldürn
Dreistein Heumatte 6
D–74731 Walldürn
Tel.: +49 6282 9238-0
Fax: +49 6282 9238-99
www.inox-color.com
(Surface treatment for stainless
steel)

Kalzip / Corus Bausysteme GmbH
August-Horch-Straße 20-22
D–56070 Koblenz
Tel.: +49 261 9834-0
Fax: +49 261 9834-100
www.kalzip.de
(Aluminium roof, wall and facade
systems)

kiener + wittlin ag
Postfach Industrie Waldeck
CH–3052 Zollikofen/Bern
Tel.: +41 31 8686111
Fax: +41 31 8694041
www.kiener-wittlin.ch
(Steel and metal, including perfo-
rated and embossed sheeting)

Koch Membranen GmbH
Nordstraße 1
D–83253 Rimsting
Tel.: +49 8051 6909-80
Fax: +49 8051 6909-19
www.kochmembranen.de
(Metal fabric, textile construction)

Lochanstalt Aherhammer
Stahlschmidt & Flender GmbH
Aherhammer 3-9
D–57223 Kreuztal
Tel.: +49 2732 5853-0
Fax: +49 2732 27544
www.aherhammer.de
(Perforated sheeting)

Mantz Industrieprodukte
Hechendorferstraße 132
D–82211 Herrsching
Tel.: +49 8152 3996-27
Fax: +49 8152 3996-28
www.mantz-online.de
(Perforated sheeting, expanded
metal, wire fabrics)

MetallPfister E. Pfister & Cie AG
Neue Winterthurerstrasse 20
CH–8305 Dietlikon
Tel.: +41 1 8335200
Fax: +41 1 8330224
www.metallpfister.ch
(Trade in perforated sheeting,
expanded metal, metal fabrics)

Metallwarenfabrik Neustadt GmbH
Industrieweg 34
D–23730 Neustadt
Tel.: +49 4561 5179-0
Fax: +49 4561 5179-25
www.mn-welltec.de
(Corrugated sheeting, perforated
sheeting, embossed sheeting)

Mevaco Holding GmbH & Co. KG
Poststraße 12
D–73033 Göppingen
Tel.: +49 7161 6105-300
Fax: +49 7161 6105-399
www.mevaco.com
(Perforated sheeting)

Michael Gompf
Edelstahlstrukturen
Raichbergstraße 36
D–72622 Nürtingen
Tel.: +49 7022 41247
Fax: +49 7022 241140
www.edelstahlstrukturen.de
(Stainless steel products)

Moradelli
Fabrik für Loch- und Prägebleche
Daimlerstraße 1
D–85551 Kirchheim b. München
Tel.: +49 89 90000-10
Fax: +49 89 9044466
www.moradelli.de
(Perforated sheeting, embossed
sheeting)

Paul Gysin AG
Fabrik für Lochbleche, Handel mit
Streckmetall
Tschertligasse 6
CH–4622 Egerkingen
Tel.: +41 62 39803-30
Fax: +41 62 39803-34
www.gysinag.ch
(Perforated sheeting, embossed
sheeting)

ProMetall GmbH
Aumühlstraße 14 (ARED-Park)
A–2544 Leobersdorf
Tel.: +43 2256 62541-0
Fax: +43 2256 62541-22
www.streckmetall.com
(Perforated sheeting, expanded
sheeting, napped sheeting, framing
units)

Rau Streckgitter GmbH
Neulandstraße 34
D–74889 Sinsheim
Tel.: +49 7261 9416-0
Fax: +49 7261 9416-16
www.rau-streckgitter.de
(Expanded grids)

RHEINZINK GmbH & Co. KG
Bahnhofstraße 90
D–45711 Datteln
Tel.: +49 2363 605-0
Fax: +49 2363 605-209
www.rheinzink.de
(Roof coverings and façade clad-
ding with folding technology)

Roland Doering Industrieprodukte
Am Bahnhof 5a
D–76297 Stutensee
Tel.: +49 7249 9473-0
Fax: +49 7249 9473-20
www.doering-roland.de
(Representatives for perforated
sheeting, expanded metal)

Schäfer Lochbleche
GmbH & Co. KG
Postfach 1120
D–57272 Neunkirchen
Tel.: +49 2735 787-05
Fax: +49 2735 787-528
www.schaefer-lochbleche.de
(Perforated sheeting)

SHS Lochbleche Butzbach GmbH
Holzheimer Straße 14-16
D–35510 Butzbach
Tel.: +49 6033 9646-0
Fax: +49 6033 9646-10
www.lochblech.de
(Perforated sheeting, embossed
sheeting)

Sorst Streckmetall GmbH
Wohlenbergstraße 11
D–30179 Hannover
Tel.: +49 511 676756-52
Fax: +49 511 676756-56
www.sorst.de
(Expanded metal)

Spörl KG
Staudenweg 13
D–72517 Sigmaringendorf
Tel.: +49 7571 73930
Fax: +49 7571 14022
www.spoerl.de
(Metal weaving for fine and ultra-fine
metal fabrics)

The Expanded Metal Company Ltd,
PO Box 14, Longhill Industrial Estate
(North), Hartlepool
GB–Cleveland TS25 1PR
Tel.: +44 1429 867388
Fax: +44 1429 866795
www.expandedmetalcompany.co.uk

Weisse & Eschrich GmbH & Co. KG
Drahtgewebefabriken
Postfach 1261
D–96334 Ludwigstadt
Tel.: +49 9263 946-0
Fax: +49 9263 946-40
www.weisse.de
(Wire fabrics)

Links/addresses:

Informationsstelle Edelstahl Rostfrei
Sohnstraße 65
D–40237 Düsseldorf
Tel.: +49 211 6707-835
Fax: +49 2 11 6707-344
www.edelstahl-rostfrei.de

Fachabteilung Lochbleche im Indus-
trieverband Stahlverarbeitung e.V.
Spandauer Straße 25
D–57072 Siegen
Tel.: +49 271 53038
Fax: +49 271 56769
www.fachabteilung-lochbleche.de

Fachverband der Metallwaren-indus-
trie Österreichs
Wiedner Hauptstraße 63
A–1045 Wien
Tel.: +43 590900-3482
Fax: +43 5051020
www.fmmi.at

Stahl-Informations-Zentrum
Postfach 10 48 42
D–40039 Düsseldorf
Tel.: +49 211 6707-846
Fax: +49 211 6707-344
www.stahl-info.de
www.stahl-online.de

Picture credits:

Black-and-white photographs at chapter heads:

Title
top: Pavillon Expo 2000, Hannover,
          Architects: SARC Architects
centre: Space for the summer, Michael Johl,
          Radoslaw Joswiak, Cosmas Ruppel
bottom: 5 Höfe, Munich, Architects: Herzog &
          de Meuron, Basel

Page 9:   Department store in Tokyo
          Material: glass blocks, custom made
          Architects: Renzo Piano Building Work-
          shop, Paris/Tokyo

Page 39: Ricola warehouse, Mulhouse
          Material: polycarbonate cellular
          sheeting, printed
          Architects: Herzog & de Meuron, Basel

Page 57: Millennium Dome, London
          Material, exterior: mid-weight, PTFE-
          coated glass fibre fabric
          Interior: light glass fibre fabric with PTFE
          coating
          Architects: Richard Rogers Partnership,
          London
          Structural engineers: Büro Happold,
          Bath
          Membrane construction: Birdair,
          New York

Page 79: "Takahashi Building", Gifu, Japan
          Material: perforated metal sheeting
          Architects: Akiko and Hiroshi Taka-
          hashi, Yokohama

Page 99: Olympic indoor swimming pool, Munich
          Material: PMMA, modified for fire
          protection
          Architets: Behnisch und Partner,
          Stuttgart Behnisch · Auer · Büxel ·
          Tränkner · Weber
          Roofing: Behnisch und Partner,
          Frei Otto, Leonhardt und Andrä

Photos without credits are from the architects' own archives or the archives of DETAIL Review of Architecture. Despite intense efforts it was not possible to identify the copyright owners of certain photos and illustrations. The rights remain unaffected, however, and we request them to contact us.

AiM, Nürtingen:
page 92 right
BASF (Schweiz) Schweiz, Zurich:
page 24 bottom
Bleda + Rosa, Moncada/Valencia:
page 51
Covertex, Obing:
pages 77 bottom, 74 top, 72 top
Denancé, Michel, Paris:
page 9
Dyneon GmbH & Co. KG, Neuss:
page 71
Emdelight GmbH, Cologne, Christian Mayer:
page 17 bottom
Esch, Hans-Georg, Henef:
page 18
F. Carl Schröter, Hamburg:
page 97 bottom left, 97 bottom centre
Fink, Dietrich, Berlin:
title centre
Gabriel, Andreas, Munich:
page 62
Galletti et Matter, Lausanne; Fausto Pluchinotta:
pages 22, 23
Gebr. Kufferath AG, Düren:
page 96 bottom
Gebr. Kufferath AG, Düren; Christian Richters:
page 94 centre
Gilbert, Dennis/View, London:
page 74 bottom
Halbe, Roland/artur, Cologne:
page 13
Halbe, Roland/Contur, Cologne:
page 88
Haver & Boecker, Oelde:
page 96 top centre
Heinrich Fiedler GmbH & Co.KG, Regensburg:
pages 90 right, 91 left, 91 centre
Heinrich, Michael, Munich:
pages 25, 89
Herzog & de Meuron, Basel:
page 78
Hirai, Hiroyuki, Tokyo:
page 55 centre
Holzherr, Florian, Munich:
page 95
Hummel, Kees, Amsterdam:
pages 85, 90 left
Ingenhousz, Bastiaan, Dordrecht:
page 55 bottom
Jocham, Margita, Munich:
pages 39, 54
Kaltenbach, Frank, Munich: title bottom,
pages 6, 17 top, 20 bottom, 40, 44–47, 52, 53, 55
top, 56 left, 77 bottom, 81, 83 centre, 83 bottom,
91 right, 94 top, 99

Kavin, Anders, Aarhus:
page 84
Kinold, Klaus, Munich:
page 63
Knott, Herbie, London:
page 76
Kramer, Luuk, Amsterdam:
page 26
Lugger, Peter, Vienna:
page 29 top
Monthiers, Jean-Marie, Paris:
page 11
Palladium Photodesign, Cologne:
page 60
Philip, Peter, Graz:
page 56 right
Pilkington GmbH, Gelsenkirchen:
page 19 bottom
Richters, Christian, Münster:
pages 59, 61
Ruault, Philippe, Nantes:
page 50
Schaum, Christine, Munich:
page 73
Schittich, Christian, Munich:
title top, pages 15, 20 top, 43, 79, 83 top
Schodder, Martin, Stuttgart:
page 17 centre
Smith, Grant, London:
page 57
Sundberg, David, New York:
page 16
Warchol, Paul, New York:
page 87
Werner, Heike, Munich:
pages 77 top, 90 centre, 92 left, 92 centre, 94 bottom, 96 top left, 96 top right, 97 top, 97 bottom right
Wessely, Heide, Munich:
pages 72 bottom, 77 centre